GUITAR CHORD SONG

TOP 100

MODERN
WORSHIP

songbook

BRENTWOOD-BENSON
music publishing

Above All

Words and Music by
PAUL BALOCHE
and LENNY LEBLANC

Melody:

A - bove all___ pow - ers,

G/B	D/C	C	Dsus	D	G	D/F♯	Em

G/D	Am7	C/G	B7sus/F♯	B7	Gmaj7/D	D7sus	D7

Verse
G/B   D/C   C   Dsus   D   G
Above all pow- ers,   above all kings,
G/B   D/C   C   Dsus   D   G
    Above all na-   ture and all   created things;
D/F♯   Em   G/D   C   G/B
Above all wisdom and all the ways of man,
Am7   C/G   D/F♯
You were here before the world began.
G   G/B   D/C   C   Dsus   D   G
    Above all king- doms,   above all thrones,
G/B   D/C   C   Dsus   D   G
    Above all won- ders the world has ever known;
D/F♯   Em   G/D   C   G/B
Above all wealth and treasures of the earth,
Am7   C/G   B7sus/F♯   B7
There's no way to measure what You're worth.

Chorus   **G**   **Am7** **D/F♯**   **G**

Crucified,   laid behind the stone;

              Am7 **D/F♯**   **G**

You lived to die,   rejected and alone;

D/F♯ **Em** **Gmaj7/D**   **C** **G/B**

Like a rose, trampled on the ground

            Am7 **G/B**

You took the fall

              C **D7sus** **D7** **G**

And thought of me   above all.

Alive, Forever, Amen

Words and Music by
TRAVIS COTTRELL,
SUE C. SMITH
and DAVID MOFFITT

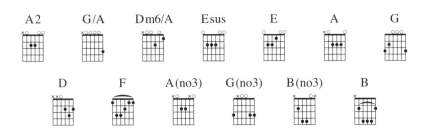

A2   **G/A**   **Dm6/A**   **Esus**   **E**   **A**   **G**

D   **F**   **A(no3)**   **G(no3)**   **B(no3)**   **B**

Verse 1

  A2   **G/A**
Let the children sing   a song of liberation.

  Dm6/A   **A2**
The God of our salvation set us free.

                   G/A
Death where is thy sting?   The curse of sin is broken;

  Dm6/A   **Esus**   **E**
The empty tomb stands open. Come and see.

Chorus

        A   **G**   **D**
He's alive, alive, alive. Hallelujah, alive.

           F   **G**   **A**
Praise and glory to the Lamb.

      A   **G**   **D**   **F**   **G**   **A**
Alive, alive, alive. Hallelujah. Alive forever. A- men.

Verse 2   **A2**
　　　Let my heart sing out,
G/A
　　　For Christ, the One and only,
Dm6/A　　　　　　　　　　**A2**
　　　　So powerful and holy, rescued me.

　　　Death won't hurt me now
G/A
　　　　Because He has redeemed me.
Dm6/A　　　　　　　　　　**Esus**　　**E**
　　　　No grave will ever keep me from my King.

Bridge   **A(no3)**
　　　Worthy is the Lamb, worthy of our praise.
G(no3)
　　　Worthy is the One who has overcome the grave.
D　　　　　　　**F**　　　　**G**
　　　Let the people dance; let the people sing.
A(no3)
　　　Worthy is the mighty King.

Bridge   **B(no3)**
(in B)
　　　Worthy is the Lamb, worthy of our praise.
A(no3)
　　　Worthy is the One who has overcome the grave.
E　　　　　　　**G**　　　　**A**
　　　Let the people dance; let the people sing.
B(no3)
　　　Worthy is the mighty King.

Tag　　**A2**　　　　**B**　　　**A2** **A** **B**
　　　　You are worthy.　　　A- men!

All Because of Jesus

Words and Music by
STEVE FEE

Melody:

Giv - er of ev - 'ry breath— I breathe,—

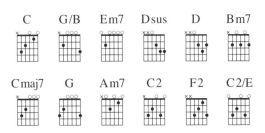

Verse

          C   **G/B**
Giver of every breath I breathe,
          C   **G/B**
Author of all eternity,
          C   **Em7**   **Dsus**   **D**
Giver of every perfect thing, to You be the glory.
          C   **G/B**
Maker of heaven and of earth,
          C   **G/B**
No one can comprehend Your worth.
          C   **Em7**   **Dsus**   **D**
King over all the universe, to You be the glory.

Pre-
Chorus
   Em7   **Bm7**   **Cmaj7**
And I'm alive because I'm alive in You.

Chorus   **G**   **Am7**   **C2**
And it's all because of Jesus I'm alive.
       G   **Am7**   **C2**
It's all because the blood of Jesus Christ
     F2   **C2/E**   **G**
That covers me and raised this dead man's life.
     F2   **C2/E**
It's all because of Jesus I'm alive.

Interlude   **C**   **G**   **C**   **G**   **C**   **Em7**   **Dsus**   **D**
               I'm alive.

Bridge   **C**   **D**   **Em7**
Every sunrise sings Your grace,
     C   **D**   **Am7**
The universe cries out Your praise.
      C   **D**   **Em7**
I'm singing freedom all my days
C   **Dsus**
Now that I'm alive.

Tag   **G**
     I'm alive.
      C   **G**
It's all because of Jesus.
      C   **G**
It's all because of Jesus.
      C   **Em7**   **Dsus** **D** **G**
It's all because of Jesus I'm alive.

All the Earth Will Sing Your Praises

Words and Music by
PAUL BALOCHE

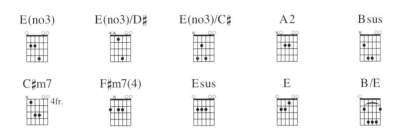

Chorus   **E(no3)**   **E(no3)/D♯**
            You lived,   You died,
E(no3)/C♯   **A2**
            You said in three days You would rise;
E(no3)   **Bsus**   **C♯m7   A2**
            You did,   You're alive.
E(no3)   **E(no3)/D♯**
            You rule,   You reign;
E(no3)/C♯   **A2**
            You said You're coming back again;
E(no3)   **Bsus**
            I know   that You will.
        C♯m7   **A2**   **E(no3)   Bsus**
And all the earth will sing Your praises;
C♯m7   A2   F♯m7(4)   **A2**
            All the earth will sing Your praises.

Interlude   **E(no3)**   **Bsus**   **C♯m7**   **A2**
                 F♯m7(4)   **A2**   **E(no3)**   **Esus**   **E**

Verse   **E(no3)**   **B/E**   **C♯m7**
              You took,   You take our sins away, O God.
             E(no3)   **B/E**   **C♯m7**
              You give,   You gave Your life away for us.
             A2   **C♯m7**
              You came down, You saved us through the cross.
             A2   **Bsus**
              Our hearts are changed because of Your great love.

Agnus Dei

Words and Music by
MICHAEL W. SMITH

A   Asus/B   A/C#   D   D2(#4)/E   D/F#   E/G#

E/A   D/A   F#m   E   Bm   E/D

Verse

A	Asus/B	A/C#	D	A/C#

Al-   le- lu- ia,

| A | Asus/B | A/C# | D | D2(#4)/E | D/F# |

Al-   le- lu-   ia,

          D2(#4)/E   D   A/C#   A

For the Lord God Almighty reigns.   *(Repeat)*

A   Asus/B   A/C#   D   D2(#4)/E   D/F#

Al-   le- lu-   ia!

Chorus

D/F#   E/G#   A

Ho-   ly,

E/A   A   D/A   A   F#m   E

Ho-   ly are You, Lord   God Almight- y.

Bm   A/C#   D   Bm   A/C#   D

Worthy is   the Lamb, worthy is   the Lamb,

     E/D   D   E/D   A

You are   ho-   ly,

E/A   A   D/A   A   F#m   E

Ho-   ly are You, Lord   God Almight- y.

Bm   A/C#   D   Bm   A/C#   D   E   A

Worthy is   the Lamb, worthy is   the Lamb, A-   men!

All Who Are Thirsty

Words and Music by
BRENTON BROWN
and GLENN ROBERTSON

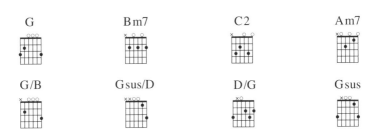

All   who   are   thirst - y,

| G | Bm7 | C2 | Am7 |

| G/B | Gsus/D | D/G | Gsus |

Verse

     G   **Bm7**
All who are thirsty, all who are weak,
     C2
Come to the fountain,
        Am7 **G/B** **C2**
Dip your heart in the stream of life.
   Gsus/D **G**   **Bm7**
Let the pain and the sorrow be washed away
       C2   **Am7** **G/B** **C2**
In the waves of His mercy, as deep cries out to deep.

Chorus 1 **Gsus/D** **G** **D/G** **Gsus** **G** **C2** **Gsus/D**
       We sing, "Come, Lord Je- sus, come. *(three times)*
       G **D/G** **Gsus** **G** **C2**
       Come, Lord Je- sus, come."

Chorus 2 **G** **D/G** **Gsus** **G** **C2**
       Ho- ly   Spir- it, come. *(three times)*

Amazing Grace
(My Chains Are Gone)

New Words and Music by
CHRIS TOMLIN and LOUIE GIGLIO

Melody:

A-maz - ing grace, how sweet the sound

D   G/D   A/D   D/F♯   G

G/B   D/A   Em7   A7

Verse 1

      D   **G/D**   **D**
Amazing grace! how sweet the sound
                A/D
That saved a wretch like me!
      D   **D/F♯** **G**   **D**
I once was lost but now I'm found;
           A/D **D**
Was blind, but now   I see.

Verse 2

          D   **G/D**   **D**
'Twas grace that taught my heart to fear,
                A/D
And grace my fears relieved.
        D   **D/F♯** **G**   **D**
How precious did that grace appear
        A/D   **D**
The hour I first believed.

Chorus

         D/F♯   **G**   **D/F♯**
My chains are gone. I've been set free.
                G/B   **D/A**
My God, my Savior has ransomed me.
         D/F♯   **G**   **D/F♯**
And like   a flood, His mercy reigns,
             Em7 **A7**   **D**
Unending love,   amazing grace.

Verse 3

         D   **G/D**   **D**
The Lord has promised good to me;
                 A/D
His word my hope secures.
         D **D/F♯**   **G**   **D**
He will my shield and portion be
         A/D   **D**
As long as life endures.

Verse 4   **G/D**   **D**   **G/D**   **D**
The earth shall soon dissolve like snow,
              A/D
The sun forbear to shine,
         D   **D/F♯**   **G**   **D**
But God, who called me here below,
         A/D **D**   **A/D** **D**
Will be forever mine, will be forever mine.
         A/D **D**
You are forever mine!

Amazed

Words and Music by
JARED ANDERSON

Melody:

You dance_____ o - ver__ me_____

D/F♯   G   A/D   G2   Asus   Em7   D

Verse

    D/F♯   G   A/D   D/F♯   G   A/D
You dance   over me while I am   una-ware.
    D/F♯   G   A/D   D/F♯   G   A/D
You sing   all around, but I   never hear the sound.

Chorus

          G2   Asus   D/F♯   G2
Lord, I'm amazed by You. Lord, I'm amazed by You.
    Em7   Asus   D
Lord, I'm amazed by You, how You love me.

Bridge

    G2   Asus   D/F♯   G2
How wide,   how deep,
    Em7   Asus   D
How great   is Your love for me.

Awesome God

Words and Music by
RICH MULLINS

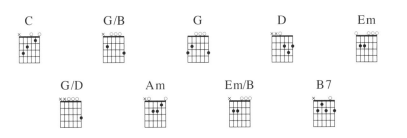

Chorus   **C**   **G/B**   **G**

Our God is an awesome God.

           D   **Em**

He reigns from heaven above

G/D **C**   **G/B**   **G**

With   wisdom, pow'r and love.

        Am   **Em/B** **B7** **Em**

Our God is an awe-   some God!

Awesome Is the Lord Most High

Words and Music by
CHRIS TOMLIN, JESSE REEVES,
JON ABEL and CARY PIERCE,

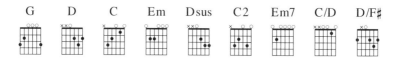

Verse 1

G   D
Great are You, Lord, mighty in strength.
C   G
You are faithful; You will ever be.
                               D
We will praise You all of our days.
C   Em
It's for Your glory we offer everything.

Half-Chorus

Dsus   G
Raise your hands, all you nations.
             C2
Shout to God, all creation.
       Em7   C2
How awesome is the Lord Most High!

Verse 2   **G**   **D**
            Where You send us, God, we will go.
            C   **G**
            And You're the answer we want the world to know.
                                            D
            We will trust You when You call our name.
            C   **Em**
            Where You lead us, we'll follow all the way.

Chorus   **Dsus**   **G**
            Raise your hands, all you nations.
                        C2
            Shout to God, all creation.
                Em7   **C2**
            How awesome is the Lord Most High!
                C/D **G**   **D/F♯**
            We will   praise You together, for now and forever.
                Em7   **C2**
            How awesome is the Lord Most High!

Bridge   **G**   **D**
            Hallelujah! Hallelujah!
                Em7   **C2**
            How awesome is the Lord Most High!
            G   **D**
            Hallelujah! Hallelujah!
                Em7   **C2**
            How awesome is the Lord Most High!

Beautiful King

Words and Music by
CHAD CATES, JONATHAN LEE and MATT UNDERWOOD

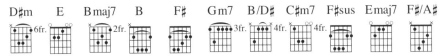

I hear a sound— like   rush-ing wa - ter.

D#m   E   Bmaj7   B   F#   G#m7   B/D#   C#m7   F#sus   Emaj7   F#/A#

Intro   **D#m   E   Bmaj7   D#m   E   Bmaj7**

Verse 1   **B   F#**
             I hear a sound like   rushing water.
             G#m7   F#
             It's growing louder,   just like thunder.

Pre-   **E   B/D#**
Chorus   This is our anthem,   our song of love.
             C#m7   B/D#   E   F#sus
             It is rising, the sound of hallelujah!

Chorus   **F#   B   F#**
             Beautiful King, wonderful Savior,
                Emaj7   B   F#
             You reign forever and ever.
                B   F#/A#   G#m7   F#   Emaj7
             O Lord, in spirit and truth, I live to sing   to You,
                            D#m   E   Bmaj7
             My beautiful King,
                            D#m   E   F#sus
             My beautiful King.

Verse 2   **B   F#**
             Clothed in splendor,   full of glory,
             G#m7   F#
             You gave Your life to   make us holy.

Beautiful One

Words and Music by
TIM HUGHES

Melody:

Won - der - ful, so won - der - ful,

G A D/F♯ Bm7 D

Verse 1
  G   A   D/F♯
  Wonderful, so wonderful, is Your unfailing love.
  G   A   Bm7
  Your cross has spoken mercy over me.
  G   A   D/F♯
  No eye has seen, no ear has heard, no heart could fully know
    G   A   D
  How glorious, how beautiful You are.

Chorus
      G A   G A
  Beautiful One I love, beautiful One I adore,
      G A   D
  Beautiful One, my soul must sing.

Verse 2
  G   A   D/F♯
  Powerful, so powerful, Your glory fills the skies,
  G   A   Bm7
  Your mighty works displayed for all to see.
  G   A D/F♯
  The beauty of Your majesty awakes my heart to sing.
    G   A   D
  How marvelous, how wonderful You are.

Bridge
    G   A
  You opened my eyes to Your wonders anew.
    G   A
  You captured my heart with this love,
    G   A   D
  'Cause nothing on earth is as beautiful as You.

Better Is One Day

Words and Music by
MATT REDMAN

Melody:

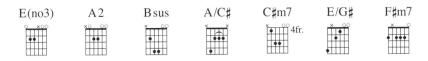

How love-ly is Your dwell-ing place,

E(no3) A2 Bsus A/C♯ C♯m7 E/G♯ F♯m7

Verse 1

     E(no3)   A2   Bsus
How lovely is Your dwelling place,   O Lord almighty.

     E(no3)   Bsus
For my soul longs and even faints for You.

     E(no3)   A2   Bsus
For here my heart is satisfied   within Your presence.

     E(no3)   Bsus
I sing beneath the shadow of Your wings.

Chorus

     A2
Better is one day in Your courts,

     Bsus
Better is one day in Your house,

     A2   A/C♯   Bsus
Better is one day in Your courts than thousands elsewhere.

     A2
Better is one day in Your courts,

     Bsus
Better is one day in Your house,

     A2   A/C♯   Bsus
Better is one day in Your courts than thousands elsewhere,

     E(no3)
Than thousands elsewhere.

Verse 2
     E(no3)   **A2**   **Bsus**
One thing I ask, and I would seek: to see Your beauty,
     E(no3)   **Bsus**
To find You in the place Your glory dwells.
     E(no3)   **A2**   **Bsus**
One thing I ask, and I would seek: to see Your beauty,
     E(no3)   **Bsus**
To find You in the place Your glory dwells.

Bridge
  C♯m7   **Bsus**
My heart and flesh cry out
A2   **Bsus**
For You, the living God.
C♯m7   **Bsus**   **A2**   **Bsus**
Your Spirit's water to my soul.
C♯m7   **Bsus**
I've tasted and I've seen.
A2
Come once again to me.
E/G♯
I will draw near to You,
F♯m7   **Bsus**
I will draw near to You, to You.

Blessed Be Your Name

Words and Music by
MATT REDMAN
and BETH REDMAN

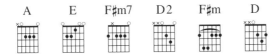

Verse 1

   A   E   F#m7   D2
     Blessed be Your name in the land that is plentiful,
         A   E
  Where Your streams of abundance flow;
     D2
  Blessed be Your name.
  A   E   F#m7   D2
    Blessed be Your name when I'm found in the desert place,
    A   E   D2
  When I walk through the wilderness; blessed be Your name.

Pre-Chorus

A	E	F#m7	D2

Every blessing You pour out I'll   turn back to praise.

A	E	F#m7	D2

When the darkness closes in, Lord,   still I will say:

Chorus

A	E		F#m D

Blessed be the name of the Lord. Blessed be Your name.

A	E

Blessed be the name of the Lord.

F#m E D

Blessed be Your glori- ous name.

Verse 2

A	E	F#m7	D2

Blessed be Your name when the sun's shining down on me,

A	E	D2

When the world's all as it should be; blessed be Your name.

A	E	F#m7	D2

Blessed be Your name on the road marked with suffering;

A	E	D2

Though there's pain in the offering, blessed be Your name.

Bridge

A	E	F#m	D

You give and take away. You give and take away.

A	E	F#m	D

My heart will choose to say, "Lord, blessed be Your name."

Breathe

Words and Music by
MARIE BARNETT

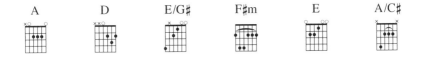

Verse

A　　　　D　　　　A　　　　　D
This is the air I breathe,　　this is the air I breathe,

A　　E/G♯　F♯m　　E　D　　A/C♯　E
Your holy　　presence　　　living　　in me.

A　　　　D　　　　A　　　　　D
This is my daily bread,　　this is my daily bread,

A　　E/G♯　F♯m　E　D　　A/C♯　　E
Your very　Word　　spoken　　to me.

Chorus

　　　A　E/G♯　F♯m　E　　　　　　D　　　F♯m　E
And I,　　　　　　　　　I'm desp'rate for You.

　　　A　E/G♯　F♯m　E　　　　　　D　　F♯m　E　(A)
And I,　　　　　　　　　I'm lost without You.

Come, Now Is the Time to Worship

Words and Music by
BRIAN DOERKSEN

Melody:

Come,   now is the time——

D	Dsus	A	Em7	G	Bm	Asus

Chorus

D   **Dsus** **D**
Come, now is the time to wor-   ship.
A   **Em7**   **G**
Come, now is the time to give your heart.
D   **Dsus** **D**
Come, just as you are, to wor-   ship.
A   **Em7**   **G**   **D**
Come, just as you are, before your God. Come.

Verse

G   **D**
One day every tongue will confess You are God,
G   **D**
One day every knee will bow.
G   **Bm**
Still, the greatest treasure remains for those
      Em7   **Asus**   **A**
Who gladly choose You now.

Days of Elijah

Words and Music by
ROBIN MARK

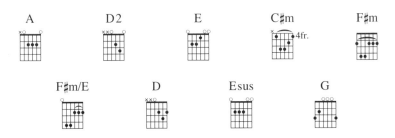

Verse 1

> A   D2 A   E   A
> These are the days of Elijah, declaring the word of the Lord.
>   D2
> And these are the days of Your servant, Moses,
> A   E   A
> Righteousness being restored.
>   C♯m   F♯m F♯m/E
> And though these are days of great trials
>   D   Esus E
> Of famine and darkness and sword,
>   A   D2
> Still we are the voice in the desert crying,
>   A   Esus E A
> "Prepare ye the way of the Lord."

Chorus   Esus   E   A   D

Behold,   He comes riding on the clouds,

                         A   E

Shining like the sun, at the trumpet call.

         Esus   E   A   D

So lift   your voice, it's the year of Jubilee,

                  A   E

And out of Zion's hill salvation comes.

Verse 2   A   D2

And these are the days of Ezekiel,

         A   E   A

The dry bones becoming as flesh.

                       D2

And these are the days of Your servant David,

         A   E   A

Rebuilding a temple of praise.

         C♯m   F♯m   F♯m/E

And these are the days of the harvest,

        D   Esus   E

The fields are as white in the world.

        A   D2

And we are the laborers in Your vineyard,

        A   Esus   E   A

Declaring the word   of the Lord.

Bridge   Esus   A   G   D   A

Who   was, and who is, and who is to come!

         A   G   D   A

Who was, and who is, and who is to come, to come, to come!

Draw Me Close

Words and Music by
KELLY CARPENTER

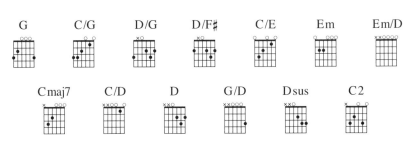

Verse
G   **C/G   D/G**   **G**
    Draw me close to You,   never let me go,
D/F♯   **C/E**   **Em**
    I lay it all down again,
Em/D   **Cmaj7**   **C/D   D**
To hear You say that I'm Your friend.
G   **C/G   D/G**   **G**
    You are my desire,   no one else will do,
D/F♯   **C/E**
    'Cause nothing else could take Your place,
Em **Em/D**   **Cmaj7**   **C/D   D**
    To feel the warmth of Your embrace.
G/D   **C/D Dsus**   **D**   **G C/D D**
    Help me find the way,   bring me back to You.

Chorus
G   **D/G   C/G   G**   **D/F♯   C/E   Dsus**
    You're all I want,   You're all I've ever needed.
G   **D/G   C/G   C2**   **D**   **G**
    You're all I want,   help me know You are near.

Everlasting God

Words and Music by
BRENTON BROWN
and KEN RILEY

Melody:

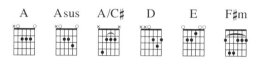

Strength will rise as we wait___ up-on the Lord.

A	A sus	A/C♯	D	E	F♯m

Verse

    A   **Asus**   **A**
Strength will rise as we wait upon the Lord.
      Asus   **A**   **Asus**   **A**
We will wait upon the Lord. We will wait upon the Lord.
                    Asus   **A**
Strength will rise as we wait upon the Lord.
      Asus   **A**   **Asus**   **A**
We will wait upon the Lord. We will wait upon the Lord.

Pre-
Chorus

A/C♯ **D** **A/C♯** **D**   **E** **F♯m** **E**
Our   God, You   reign for- ev-   er,
A/C♯ **D** **A/C♯** **D**   **E** **F♯m** **E**
Our   hope, our   strong De- liv- 'rer.

Chorus

A   **A/C♯** **D**   **F♯m**
You are the everlasting   God, the everlasting God.
                    D
You do not faint; You won't grow weary.
A   **A/C♯** **D**
You're the Defender of the   weak;
              F♯m
You comfort those in need.
            D   **(A)**
You lift us up on wings like eagles.

Enough

Words and Music by
CHRIS TOMLIN
and LOUIE GIGLIO

Melody:

All of You— is more than e-nough

G	C/E	Dsus	C2	C	G/B	Am7

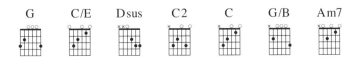

Chorus

       G   C/E   Dsus   C2   G
All of You is more than enough for   all of me,
C/E   Dsus   C2   G
For every thirst and   every need.
C/E   Dsus   C   G/B
You satisfy   me   with Your love,
     C2   Dsus   G
And all I have in You is more than enough.
C/E Dsus C2 G C/E Dsus C2

Verse 1

    G   C2   Dsus G/B   C2
You're my supply, my breath of life;
      Am7   Dsus
Still more awesome than I know.
    G   C2 Dsus   G/B C2
You're my reward, worth living for;
      Am7   Dsus
Still more awesome than I know.

Verse 2   **G**   **C2** **Dsus** **G/B**   **C2**

You're my sacri-fice of greatest price;

           Am7   **Dsus**

Still more awesome than I know.

G   **C2**   **Dsus**   **G/B** **C2**

You're my coming King, You are every- thing;

           Am7   **Dsus**

Still more awesome than I know.

Bridge   **G**   **C2** **Dsus**   **C2** **G/B**

More than all I want, more than all I need,

C2   **Dsus**

You are more than enough for me.

G   **C2** **Dsus**   **C2**   **G/B**

More than all I know, more than all I can see.

C2   **Dsus**

You are more than enough.

Everyday

Words and Music by
JOEL HOUSTON

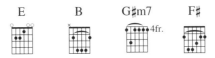

E   B   G#m7   F#

Verse 1

   E   B   G#m7   F#
What to say, Lord? It's You who gave me life,
      E   B   G#m7   F#
And I can't explain just how much You mean to me
E   B   G#m7
Now that You have saved me, Lord.
        F#   E
I give all that I am to You,
         B G#m7 F#   E
That every-day I can be a light that shines Your name.
B G#m7 F# E B G#m7 F#

Verse 2

   E   B   G#m7   F#   E
Every-day, Lord, I'll learn to stand upon Your Word.
      B   G#m7   F#   E
And I pray that I, that I may come to know You more,
        B   G#m7   F#
That You would guide me in every single step I take,
     E   B G#m7   F#   B
That   every-day I can be Your light unto the world.

Chorus   **(B)**   **E**   **G♯m7** **F♯**

          Every-day, it's You I'll live for.

     B   **E**   **G♯m7** **F♯**   **B**

       Every-day, I'll follow after You.

            E   **G♯m7**   **F♯**   **B** **E** **G♯m7** **F♯**

Every-day, I'll walk with You, my Lord.

(repeat)

Bridge   **B**   **E**   **G♯m7** **F♯**

It's You I live for every- day.

         B   **E**   **G♯m7** **F♯**

It's You I live for every- day.

         B   **E**   **G♯m7** **F♯** **B** **E** **G♯m7** **F♯**

It's You I live for every- day.

Every Move I Make

Words and Music by
DAVID RUIS

Melody:

La la la la la la la,   La la la la la la la!

G   C   D   Dsus   Am7   Bm7   D7sus

Intro   G   C   D   C   (G)
La la la la la la la, La la la la la la la!

Verse   G   C   Dsus
Every move I make, I make in You,
                    C
You make me move, Jesus.
G   C   Dsus   C
Every breath I take, I breathe in You.
G   C   Dsus   C
Every step I take, I take in You, You are my way, Jesus.
G   C   Dsus   C
Every breath I take, I breathe in You.

Chorus   G   Am7 Bm7   C   D7sus
Waves of mercy, waves of grace,
G   Am7   Bm7 C   D7sus   G
Everywhere I look,   I see Your   face.
        Am7   Bm7   C   D7sus
Your love has captured me.
G   Am7   Bm7
O, my God, this love,
      C   D7sus G   C   D   C   G   C   D   C
How can it   be?

Famous One

Words and Music by
CHRIS TOMLIN
and JESSE REEVES

Melody:

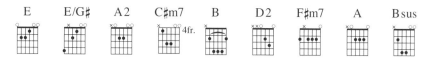

You____ are the Lord,___

E   E/G♯   A2   C♯m7   B   D2   F♯m7   A   Bsus

Chorus

E   E/G♯   A2
You are the Lord, the famous One, famous One;
C♯m7   B   A2
Great is Your name in all   the earth.
     E   E/G♯   A2
The heavens declare You're glorious, glorious;
C♯m7   B   E   (D2   A2)
Great is Your fame beyond   the earth.

Verse 1

      F♯m7   C♯m7
And for all You've done and yet to do,
   A   E
With every breath I'm praising You.
   F♯m7   C♯m7
Desire of nations and every heart,
   A2   Bsus
You alone are God, You alone are God.

Verse 2

      F♯m7   C♯m7
The Morning Star is shining through,
   A   E
And every eye is watching You.
   F♯m7   C♯m7
Reveal Thy nature and miracles.
   A2   Bsus
You are beautiful, You are beautiful.

Forever

Words and Music by
CHRIS TOMLIN

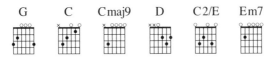

Verse 1

   G
Give thanks to the Lord our God and King;

His love endures forever.
C
For He is good, He is above all things;
 Cmaj9   **G**
His love endures forever.

Pre-
Chorus
   D   **C2/E**
Sing praise, sing praise.

Verse 2 **G**
 With a mighty hand and outstretched arm;

His love endures forever.
C
 For the life that's been reborn;
 Cmaj9   **G**
His love endures forever.

Chorus   **G**   **Em7**

Forever God is faithful, forever God is strong,

      D   **C**

Forever God is with us, forever.

      G   **Em7**

Forever God is faithful, forever God is strong,

      D   **C**   **G**

Forever God is with us, forever. Forever.

Verse 3   **G**

From the rising to the setting sun

His love endures forever.

           C

And by the grace of God we will carry on;

  Cmaj9   **G**

His love endures forever.

From the Inside Out

Words and Music by
JOEL HOUSTON

Melody:

A thou - sand times, I've failed;

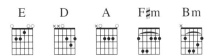

Verse 1

       E   **D**
A thousand times, I've failed;
         A   **E**
Still Your mercy remains.
          D
And should I stumble again,
       A   **E**
Still I'm caught in Your grace.
  F♯m   **D**   **A**   **E**
Everlasting, Your light will shine when all else fades.
  F♯m   **D**   **A**   **E**
Never ending, Your glory goes beyond all fame.

Verse 2
```
D  A  E  D  A  E          D
                  Your will, above all else,
      A        E
My purpose remains,
           D
The art of losing myself
      A        E
In bringing You praise.
      F♯m        D              A    E
Everlasting, Your light will shine when all else fades.
      F♯m          D        A      E
Never ending, Your glory goes beyond all fame.
```

Chorus
```
D                    A                      F♯m
      In my heart, in my soul, Lord I give You control.
                        E            D
Consume me from the inside out, Lord.
           F♯m                    E
Let justice and praise become my embrace,
                     Bm
To love You from the inside out.
```

Bridge
```
      F♯m        D              A    E
Everlasting, Your light will shine when all else fades.
      F♯m          D        A      E
Never ending, Your glory goes beyond all fame.
           A      D      E      F♯m
And the cry of my heart is to bring You praise,
           D    E          D    E  D
From the inside out. Lord, my soul cries out.
```

Friend of God

Words and Music by
MICHAEL GUNGOR and
ISRAEL HOUGHTON

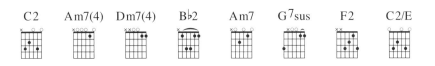

Verse

C2   **Am7(4)**
Who am I that You are mindful of me?
     Dm7(4)   **C2**
That You hear me when I call?
                              Am7(4)
Is it true that You are thinking of me?
     Dm7(4)   **B♭2**
How You love me, it's amazing.

Chorus

C2   **Am7**
I am a friend of God. I am a friend of God.
Dm7(4)   **G7sus**   **C2**
I am a friend of God, He calls me friend.
C2   **Am7**
I am a friend of God. I am a friend of God.
Dm7(4)   **G7sus**   **C2**
I am a friend of God, He calls me friend.

Bridge

F2   **C2/E**   **Dm7(4)**   **F2**
God Almighty, Lord of Glory, You have called me friend.
F2   **C2/E**   **Dm7(4)**   **F2**
God Almighty, Lord of Glory, You have called me friend.

Give Us Clean Hands

Words and Music by
CHARLIE HALL

Capo 1st fret and play in G

G	D	G/B	C	C/D	Em

Verse

G   D   G/B
We bow our hearts;   we bend our knees.
C   G C/D
Oh Spirit, come make us humble.
G   D   G/B
We turn our eyes   from evil things.
C
Oh Lord, we cast down our idols.

Chorus

                 G   D
Give us clean hands; give us pure hearts.
            G   C
Let us not lift our souls to another.
                 G   D
Give us clean hands; give us pure hearts.
           Em   D   G
Let us not lift our souls to another.

                                       D
And, oh God, let us be a generation that seeks,
                   Em D   G
That seeks Your face, oh God of Jacob.
                                     D
And, oh God, let us be a generation that seeks,
                   Em D   C   G
That seeks Your face, oh God of Jacob.

God of This City

Words and Music by
AARON BOYD, ANDREW McCANN,
IAN JORDAN, PETER COMFORT,
PETER KERNAGHAN
and RICHARD BLEAKLEY

Melody:

You're the God of this— cit-y.

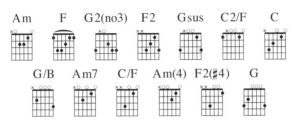

Am   F   G2(no3)   F2   Gsus   C2/F   C

G/B   Am7   C/F   Am(4)   F2(♯4)   G

Verse 1

                    Am
You're the God of this city. You're the King of these people.
                          F
You're the Lord of this nation. You are.
                    Am
You're the Light in this darkness.
                    Am
You're the hope to the hopeless.
                      F
You're the peace to the restless. You are.

**Pre-
Chorus**

    Am   **G2(no3)**   **F**   **F2**
For there is no one like our God.
Am   **G2(no3)**   **F**   **Gsus**
There is no one like You, God.

Chorus 1   **C2/F**
Greater things have yet to come
        Gsus
And greater things have still to be done
      C   **G/B**   **Am7**
In this city.
C/F
Greater things have yet to come
       Gsus   **Am7**
And greater things have still to be done here.

Verse 2   **Am**   **Am(4)**
          You're the Lord of creation, the Creator of all things.
                          Am   **F2   F2(♯4)**
          You're the King above all kings. You are.
                          Am
          You're the strength in our weakness.
                          Am(4)
          You're the love to the broken.
                          Am   **F2   F2(♯4)**
          You're the joy in the sadness. You are.

Chorus 2   **F2**
          Greater things have yet to come
                  Gsus
          And greater things have still to be done
              C   **G/B   Am7**
          In this city.
                  F2
          Where glory shines from hearts alive
                  Gsus
          With praise for You and love for You
              C   **G/B   Am7**
          In this city.
          F2
          Greater things have yet to come
                  Gsus
          And greater things have still to be done
              C   **G/B   Am7   G**
          In this city.
          F2
          Greater things have yet to come
                  Gsus   **Am**
          And greater things have still to be done here.

God of Wonders

Words and Music by
STEVE HINDALONG
and MARC BYRD

Lord of all___ cre - a - tion,___

Dsus Em7 C2 G D

Am9 Am7 Cmaj9 C D2(add4)

Verse 1

Dsus Em7 C2 Dsus Em7   C2
  Lord of all creation, of water, earth and sky,

Dsus   Em7   C2
  The heavens are Your tabernacle;

Dsus   Em7   C2
  Glory to the Lord on high.

Chorus

G   Dsus D
God of wonders beyond our galaxy,

    Am9 Am7 Cmaj9 C
You are ho- ly, ho- ly;

  G   Dsus D
The universe declares Your majesty,

    Am9 Am7 Cmaj9 C
You are ho- ly, ho- ly;

C D2(add4) C   D2(add4) C
Lord of heaven and earth, Lord of heaven and earth.

Verse 2   **Dsus**   **Em7**   **C2**
                      Early in the morning
             Dsus   **Em7**   **C2**
                      I will celebrate the light.
             Dsus   **Em7**   **C2**
                      When I stumble in the darkness
             Dsus   **Em7**   **C2**
                      I will call Your name by night.

Bridge   **Am7**   **C2**   **Dsus**
                      Hallelujah to the Lord of heaven and earth,
             Am7   **C2**   **Dsus**
                      Hallelujah to the Lord of heaven and earth,
             Am7   **C2**   **Dsus**   **G**
                      Hallelujah to the Lord of heaven and earth!

Grace Like Rain

Words and Music by
TODD AGNEW
and CHRIS COLLINS
(Original lyrics to
"Amazing Grace"
by John Newton)

Melody:

A - maz - ing Grace, — how sweet

Dm   B♭   F   C

Verse 1

    Dm   B♭   F   C
Amazing Grace, how sweet the sound
    Dm   B♭   F C
That saved a wretch like me.
    Dm   B♭   F   C
I once was lost but now am found,
      Dm   B♭   F   C
Was blind, but now, I see so clearly.

Chorus

    Dm   B♭   F   C
Hallelujah, Grace like rain falls down on me.
Dm   B♭   F   C
Hallelujah, and all my stains are washed away,
        Dm B♭ F C
They're washed away.

Verse 2

      Dm   B♭   F   C
'Twas Grace that taught my heart to fear
    Dm   B♭   F   C
And Grace my fears relieved.
     Dm   B♭   F   C   Dm B♭   F   C
How precious did that Grace appear the hour I first believed.

Verse 3

      Dm   B♭   F   C
When we've been there ten thousand years
     Dm   B♭   F C
Bright shining as the sun
     Dm   B♭   F   C
We've no less days to sing Your praise
    Dm   B♭   C
Than when we've first begun.

Hallelujah

(Your Love Is Amazing)

Words and Music by
BRENTON BROWN and
BRIAN DOERKSEN

Melody:

Your love is a-maz - ing,

G/B   C2   Dsus   G   Em7

Verse 1

      G/B   C2
Your love is amazing, steady and unchanging.
           Dsus   C2
Your love is a mountain firm beneath my feet.
           G/B   C2
Your love is a mystery, how You gently lift me.
           Dsus   C2
When I am surrounded Your love carries me.

Chorus   G   Dsus   Em7   C2
Hallelujah, hallelujah, hallelujah, Your love makes me sing.
                  G   Dsus   Em7   C2
Hallelujah, hallelujah, hallelujah, Your love makes me sing.

Verse 2   G/B   C2
Your love is surprising. I can feel it rising,
                    Dsus   C2
All the joy that's growing deep inside of me.
            G/B   C2
Every time I see You all Your goodness shines through.
           Dsus   C2
I can feel this God song rising up in me.

Tag   C2   G
Lord, You make me sing. How You make me sing.

Happy Day

Words and Music by
TIM HUGHES
and BEN CANTELON

Melody:

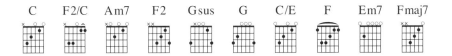

The great-est day in his - to - ry,

C   F2/C   Am7   F2   Gsus   G   C/E   F   Em7   Fmaj7

Verse 1

  C
    The greatest day in history,
  F2/C
     Death is beaten; You have rescued me.
  Am7   **F2**
     Sing it out: Jesus is alive!
  C
     The empty cross, the empty grave,
  F2
     Life eternal, You have won the day.
  Am7   **F2**   **Gsus**
     Shout it out: Jesus is alive! He's alive!

Chorus

       C   **F2**   **Am7**
  And oh, happy day, happy day,
         G
  When You washed my sin away.
       C   **F2**   **Am7**
  And oh, happy day, happy day,
       G
  No, I'll never be the same.

Interlude **C/E** **F2**   **Am7**   **G**
      Forever I am changed.   Forever I'm changed.

Verse 2   **C**

       When I stand in that place,

    F

       Free at last, meeting face to face,

    Am7   **F2**

       I am Yours; Jesus, You are mine!

    C

       Endless joy, perfect peace,

    F2

       Earthly pain finally will cease.

    Am7   **F2**   **Gsus**

       Celebrate: Jesus is alive! He's alive!

Coda   **C/E**   **F2**   **Am7**

            No, no, no,

     G   **C/E** **F2** **Am7** **G**

    Forever I am changed.

Bridge   **Am7**   **Em7**

    Oh, what a glorious day,

             Fmaj7

    What a glorious way, my Lord

       C

    That You have saved me.

       Am7   **Em7**

    And oh, what a glorious day,

            Fmaj7   **C**

    What a glorious name: Jesus, Savior!

Tag   **C/E** **F2** **Am7**   **G**   **C/E**

          No, no, no, forever I am changed.

    F2   **Am7**

       I'll never be the same.   I'll never be the same.

    G   **F2**   **C**

       I'll never be the same.

He Reigns

Words and Music by
PETER FURLER
and STEVE TAYLOR

Melody:

It's the song of the — re - deemed —

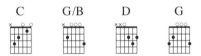

Verse 1

     C   **G/B**   **D**
It's the song of the redeemed rising from the African plain.
     C   **G/B**   **D**
It's the song of the forgiven drowning out the Amazon rain.
      C   **G/B**   **D**
The song of Asian believers filled with God's holy fire.
         C
It's every tribe, every tongue, every nation,
 G/B   **D**
A love song born of a grateful choir.

GUITAR CHORD SONGBOOK

Chorus

                                      C
It's all God's children singing, "Glory, glory,
G   **D**
Hallelujah! He reigns, He reigns!"
                                        C
It's all God's children singing, "Glory, glory,
G   **D**
Hallelujah! He reigns, He reigns!"

Verse 2

          C
Let it rise above the four winds,
G/B   **D**
Caught up in the heavenly sound.
                               C
Let praises echo from the towers of cathedrals
       G/B   **D**
To the faithful gathered underground.
                             C
Of all the songs sung from the dawn of creation,
G/B   **D**
Some were meant to persist.
                         C
Of all the bells rung from a thousand steeples,
G/B   **D**
None rings truer than this:

Bridge

            C
And all the powers of darkness
G   **D**
Tremble at what they've just heard,
              C
'Cause all the powers of darkness
G   **D**
Can't drown out a single word.

Here I Am to Worship

Words and Music by
TIM HUGHES

Melody:

Light of the World, You stepped down

E   Bsus   F♯m   A2

B7sus   B/D♯   E/G♯   A

Verse 1

E   **Bsus**   **F♯m**
Light of the World, You stepped down into darkness,
E   **Bsus**   **A2**
Opened my eyes, let me see.
E   **Bsus**   **F♯m**
Beauty that made this heart adore You,
E   **Bsus**   **A2**
Hope of a life spent with You.

Chorus

B7sus   **E**   **B/D♯**
So, here I am   to worship, here I am to bow down,
       E/G♯   **A2**
Here I am to say that You're my God.
           E   **B/D♯**
You're altogether lovely, altogether worthy,
       E/G♯   **A2**   **B7sus** **(E)**
Altogether wonderful to me.

Verse 2   **E**   **Bsus**   **F♯m**

King of all days, oh so highly exalted,

E   **Bsus**   **A2**

Glorious in heaven above.

E   **Bsus**   **F♯m**

Humbly You came to the earth You created,

E   **Bsus**   **A2**

All for love's sake became poor.

Bridge   **B/D♯** **E/G♯**   **A**

And I'll never   know how much it cost

B/D♯ **E/G♯** **A**

To see my sin   upon that cross.

Here Is Our King

Words and Music by
DAVID CROWDER

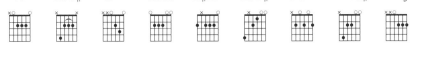

Chorus

      A   **A/C♯**
Here is our King. Here is our Love.
      D2   **A**
Here is our God who's come to bring us back to Him.
      A/C♯ **D2**
He is the One. He is Jesus.
        A   **A/C♯**
And He is our King. He is our Love.
     D2   **A**
He is our God who's come to bring us back to Him.
      A/C♯ **D2**
He is the One. He is Jesus, Jesus.

Verse 1 **A/C♯**   **D2**   **A/C♯**   **D2**
     From wherever spring arrives to heal the ground,
A/C♯   **D2**   **A/C♯**   **D2**
     From wherever searching comes, the look itself,
A/C♯   **D2**   **A/C♯**
     A trace of what we're looking for.
     D2   **A/C♯** **D2**
So be quiet now and wait.

Pre-Chorus	**Esus**		**D2**	**Esus**		**D2**	**Esus**

Pre-
Chorus

Esus   **D2** **Esus**   **D2** **Esus**
    The ocean   is growing;
    D2
The tide is coming in. Here it is.

Verse 2

A/C♯   **D2**   **A/C♯**   **D2**
    And what was said to the rose to make it unfold,
A/C♯   **D2**   **A/C♯**
    Was said to me here in my chest.
    D2   **A/C♯** **D2** **A/C♯**
So be quiet now and rest.
    D2   **A/C♯** **D2**
So be quiet now and rest.

Tag

F♯m7 **E/G♯** **A** **Bm7** **A2/C♯** **Dmaj7**
Maj-   es-   ty, fi-   nal-   ly.
F♯m7 **E/G♯** **A** **Bm7** **A2/C♯** **Dmaj7** **A**
Maj-   es-   ty, fi-   nal-   ly here.

He Knows My Name

Words and Music by
TOMMY WALKER

Melody:

I have a Mak- er,

E   F♯m7   E/G♯   A   E/B

B   B7sus   Esus/F♯   C♯m7   4fr.

Verse 1

E   F♯m7   E/G♯   A   E/B   B   B7sus
   I have a Mak- er,   He formed my heart.

E   F♯m7   E/G♯   A
   Before even time began

   E/B   B   B7sus   E   Esus/F♯   E/G♯
My life was in   His   hands.

Chorus

A   E   B   E   A   E   B   E
   He knows my name.   He knows my every thought.

A   E   B   C♯m7   F♯m7   B   E
   He sees each tear that falls, and hears me when I call.

(B7sus - *1st time*)   **(Esus/F♯   E/G♯** - *2nd time*)

Verse 2

E   F♯m7   E/G♯   A   E/B   B   B7sus
   I have a Fa-   ther,   He calls me His own.

E   F♯m7   E/G♯   A
   He'll never   leave   me

   E/B   B   B7sus   E   Esus/F♯   E/G♯
No matter where I   go.

Tag

   A   B   C♯m7   F♯m7   B   E
He hears me when I call, And He hears me when I call.

Holy Is the Lord

Words and Music by
CHRIS TOMLIN
and LOUIE GIGLIO

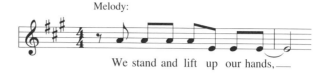

Melody:

We stand and lift up our hands, ——

A   D2   Esus   A/C♯   B7   F♯m7   E   E/G♯   G2   D

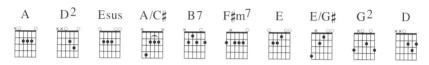

Verse

   A   D2 Esus
We stand and lift up our hands,
    A/C♯ D2   Esus
For the joy of the Lord is our strength.
   A   D2 Esus
We bow down and worship Him now.
    A/C♯ D2   Esus
How great, how awesome is He!

Pre-Chorus

        B7 D2   B7   D2
And together we sing; everyone sing:

Chorus

     A/C♯ D2 Esus
"Holy is the Lord God Almighty!
   F♯m7 D2   E
The earth is filled with His glory.
     A/C♯ D2 Esus
Holy is the Lord God Almighty!
   F♯m7 D2   Esus
The earth is filled with His glory.
   F♯m7 D2   Esus E
The earth is filled with His glory."

Bridge

      A   E/G♯
And it's rising up all around.
   G2   D
It's the anthem of the Lord's renown.

Hosanna

Words and Music by
BROOKE FRASER

Melody:

I see the King of ___ Glo - ry

Em   G   Am7   Bm7   Em7   D   G/B   C

Intro   **Em   G   Am7   Bm7**
              Em   G   Am7   Bm7

Verse 1   **G**   **Em7**
            I see the King of Glory coming on the clouds with fire.
                 Am7   **D**
            The whole earth shakes. The whole earth shakes.
            G   **Em7**
            I see His love and mercy washing over all our sin.
                Am7   **D**
            The people sing. The people sing.

Chorus   **G/B   C   D   Em7**
            Hosanna,   hosan- na,
              C   **Em7**   **D**
            Hosanna in the highest.
            G/B   C   D   Em7
            Hosanna,   hosan- na,
              C   **D**   **Em7**
            Hosanna in the high-est.

Verse 2   **G**   **Em7**
             I see a generation rising up to take their place
                         Am7   **D**
             With selfless faith, selfless faith.
             G   **Em7**
             I see a near revival stirring as we pray and seek.
                         Am7   **D**
             We're on our knees, on our knees.

Bridge   **C**   **D**
             Heal my heart and make it clean.
             G   **Em7**
             Open up my eyes to the things unseen.
             C   **D**   **Em7**
             Show me how to love like You have loved   me.

Tag   **C**   **D**   **G**   **Em7**   **C**   **G**
             Hosanna in the high-est.

How Can I Keep from Singing?

Words and Music by
CHRIS TOMLIN, MATT REDMAN
and ED CASH

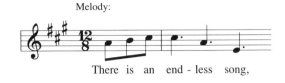

Melody:

There is an end-less song,

A	E/G♯	F♯m7	D	E	A/C♯	Bm7

Verse 1

        A   E/G♯
There is an endless song, echoes in my soul,
  F♯m7   D
I hear the music ring.
            E   A   E/G♯
And though the storms may come, I am holding on,
F♯m7   A/C♯   D
To the Rock I   cling.

Chorus

    A   E/G♯
How can I keep from singing Your praise?
        D   A/C♯   D   E
How can I ever say enough, how amazing is Your love?
A   E/G♯
How can I keep from shouting Your name?
        D   A/C♯
I know I am loved by the King,
        D   E   A
And it makes my heart want to sing.

Verse 2

        A   **E/G♯**
I will lift my eyes in the darkest night,
       F♯m7   **D**
For I know my Savior lives.
         E **A**   **E/G♯**
And I will walk with You, knowing You see me through,
       F♯m7   **A/C♯** **D**
And sing the songs You   give.

Bridge

       Bm7   **A/C♯**   **D**   **E**
I can sing in the troubled times, sing when I win.
       Bm7   **A/C♯**   **D**   **E**
I can sing when I lose my step and I fall down again.
       Bm7   **A/C♯**   **D**   **E**
I can sing 'cause You pick me up, sing 'cause You're there.
       Bm7   **A/C♯**
I can sing 'cause You hear me Lord,
       D   **E**
When I call to You in prayer.
       Bm7   **A/C♯**   **D**   **E**
I can sing 'til my last breath, sing for I know
        Bm7   **A/C♯**
That I'll sing with the angels
        D   **E**
And the saints around the throne.

How Deep the Father's Love for Us

Words and Music by
STUART TOWNEND

Melody:

How deep the Fa-ther's love for us,

E   F♯m   E/G♯   A   E/B

B   C♯m   A/C♯   A2

Verse 1

          E   **F♯m E/G♯ A**
How deep the Father's love   for   us,

       E/G♯   **E/B B**
How vast beyond all meas-   ure

          E   **F♯m E/G♯ A**
That He should give His on-   ly   Son

       E/G♯   **B E**
To make a wretch His treasure.

                  F♯m E/G♯ A
How great the pain of sear- ing   loss.

       E/G♯   **C♯m B**
The Father turns His face away

         E   **F♯m E/G♯ A**
As wounds which mar the Cho- sen   One

       E/G♯   **B E A/C♯ E/B E A2**
Bring many sons to glo-ry.

Verse 2

     E   F♯m   E/G♯ A
Behold the Man upon   a   cross,

     E/G♯   E/B   B
My sin upon His shoul- ders.

     E   F♯m   E/G♯ A
Ashamed, I hear my mock- ing   voice

     E/G♯   B   E
Call out among the scoffers.

                     F♯m   E/G♯ A
It was my sin that held   Him   there

     E/G♯   C♯m   B
Until it was accom-   plished;

     E   F♯m   E/G♯ A
His dying breath has brought me   life.

     E/G♯   B   E   A/C♯ E/B E A2
I know that it is fin- ished.

Verse 3

     E   F♯m   E/G♯ A
I will not boast in an-   y-   thing:

     E/G♯   E/B   B
No gifts, no pow'r, no wis-   dom.

     E   F♯m   E/G♯ A
But I will boast in Je-   sus   Christ:

     E/G♯   B   E
His death and resurrec- tion.

                        F♯m   E/G♯ A
Why should I gain from His   re-   ward?

     E/G♯   C♯m   B
I cannot give an an-   swer.

     E   F♯m   E/G♯ A
But this I know with all   my   heart:

     E/G♯   B   E
His wounds have paid my ran- som.

Hosanna
(Praise Is Rising)

Words and Music by
PAUL BALOCHE
and BRENTON BROWN

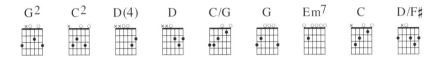

G2   C2   D(4)   D   C/G   G   Em7   C   D/F♯

Verse 1

G2   C2   G2
Praise is rising, eyes are turning to You. We turn to You.
                                    C2   G2
Hope is stirring, hearts are yearning for You. We long for You.

Pre-Chorus

          D(4)   C2   G2
'Cause when we see You, we find strength to face the day.
          D(4)   C2   G2   D
In Your presence, all our fears are washed away, washed away.

Chorus

          C/G   G   Em7   C
Hosan- na! Hosan- na!
                    G   D/F♯   Em7   C
You are the God who saves us, worthy of all our praises.
          C/G   G   Em7   C
Hosan- na! Hosan- na!
                    G   D
Come, have Your way among us.
                    Em7   C
We welcome You here, Lord Jesus.

Verse 2

G2   C2   G2
Hear the sound of hearts returning to You. We turn to You.
                                    C2
In Your kingdom, broken lives are renewed.
          G2
You make us new.

How Great Is Our God

Words and Music by
CHRIS TOMLIN, ED CASH
and JESSE REEVES

Melody:

The splen-dor of_____ the King——

C2   Am7   F2   G

Verse 1
  C2   **Am7**
The splendor of the King clothed in majesty,
    F2
Let all the earth rejoice, let all the earth rejoice.
  C2   **Am7**
He wraps Himself in light and darkness tries to hide.
    F2
It trembles at His voice, it trembles at His voice.

Chorus
  C2
How great is our God!
    Am7
Sing with me, how great is our God!
      F2 **G** **C2**
And all will see how great, how great is our God.

Verse 2 **C2**   **Am7**
Age to age, He stands and time is in His hands,
    F2
Beginning and the End, Beginning and the End.
  C2   **Am7**
The Godhead, three in one, Father, Spirit, Son,
    F2
The Lion and the Lamb, the Lion and the Lamb.

Bridge **C2**   **Am7**
Name above all names, worthy of all praise,
   F2   **G** **C2**
My heart will sing. How great is our God!

Hungry
(Falling on My Knees)

Words and Music by
KATHRYN SCOTT

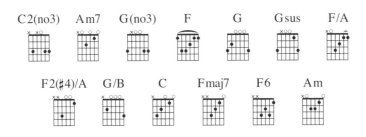

Verse 1

C2(no3)   **Am7**   **G(no3)**   **F**
Hungry, I come to You, for I know You satisfy.
C2(no3) **Am7**   **G(no3)**   **F**
I am empty, but I know Your love does not run dry.

Pre-Chorus

     G Gsus   **F/A F2(♯4)/A F/A G/B**   **F**
So I wait   for You.   So I wait for You.

Chorus

       C   **Fmaj7 F6 C**   **Fmaj7 F6**
I'm falling on my knees,   offering all of me.
      C   **Fmaj7 F6 C Am G(no3) F**
Jesus, You're all this heart is living for.

Verse 2

C2(no3)   **Am7**   **G(no3)**   **F**
Broken, I run to You, for Your arms are open wide;
C2(no3)   **Am7**   **G(no3)**   **F**
I am weary, but I know Your touch restores my life.

I Am Free

Words and Music by
JON EGAN

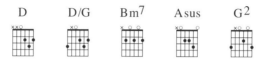

Verse   **D**
　　　　Through You the blind will see.

Through You the mute will sing.
D/G
　　　　Through You the dead will rise.

Through You all hearts will praise.
Bm7
　　　　Through You the darkness flees.
Asus　　　　　　　　　　　　　**D**
　　　　Through You my heart screams, "I am free!"

Chorus   **D**
I am free to run. (I am free to run.)
　　　G2
I am free to dance. (I am free to dance.)
　　　Bm7　　　　　　　　**Asus**
I am free to live for You. (I am free to live for You.)
　　　D
I am free! (I am free!)

I Could Sing of Your Love Forever

Words and Music by
MARTIN SMITH

Melody:

O - ver the moun - tains and the sea

E   F#m7(add4)   A2   Bsus   E/G#

Verse   E   F#m7(add4)
       Over the mountains and the sea

       Your river runs with love for me,
       A2   **Bsus**
       And I will open up my heart and let the Healer set me free.
       E   **F#m7(add4)**
       I'm happy to be in the truth, and I will daily lift my hands
       A2   **Bsus**
       For I will always sing of when Your love came down. Yeah!

Chorus   E   F#m7(add4)
       I could sing of Your love forever,
       A2   **Bsus**
       I could sing of Your love forever.

Bridge   F#m7(add4)   E/G#
       O I feel like dancing.
       A2   **Bsus**
       It's foolishness, I know.
       F#m7(add4)   **E/G#**
       But when the world has seen the light
       A2   **Bsus**
       They will dance with joy like we're dancing now.

I Give You My Heart

Words and Music by
REUBEN MORGAN

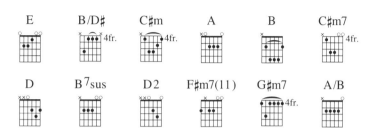

This is my — de - si - re, —

E   B/D♯   C♯m   A   B   C♯m7

D   B7sus   D2   F♯m7(11)   G♯m7   A/B

Verse

E   B/D♯ C♯m   A   E   B
This is my de-   sire, to hon-or   You.

C♯m7   B/D♯ E   D   A   B7sus
Lord, with all my   heart I worship You.

E   B/D♯ C♯m   A   E   B
With all I have with-   in me, I give You praise.

C♯m7   B/D♯ E   D2   D   A   B7sus
All that I a-   dore is in You.

Chorus

E   B   F♯m7(11)
Lord, I give You my heart, I give You my soul.

B7sus   E
I live for You alone.

B/D♯   F♯m7(11)
Every breath that I take, every moment I'm awake,

B7sus   E   (G♯m7   A/B)
Lord, have Your way in me.

In Christ Alone

Words and Music by
KEITH GETTY and
STUART TOWNEND

Melody:

In Christ a - lone my hope is found,

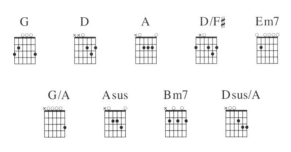

G   D   A   D/F♯   Em7

G/A   Asus   Bm7   Dsus/A

Verse 1

      G   D   G   A
In Christ alone my hope is found,

D/F♯   G   D/F♯ Em7 G/A   D
He is my light, my   strength,   my song;

      G   D   G   A
This Corner-stone, this solid Ground,

D/F♯   G D/F♯ Em7 G/A   D
Firm through the fierc-est   drought   and storm.

      D/F♯   G   D/F♯ Asus   A
What heights of love, what depths of peace,

      D/F♯   G   Bm7   Asus   A
When fears are stilled, when strivings cease!

      G   D   G   A
My Comfort-er, my All in All,

D/F♯   G D/F♯ Em7 G/A   D Dsus/A D
Here in the love of   Christ   I stand.

Verse 2

       G   **D**   **G**   **A**

In Christ alone!– who took on flesh,

D/F♯   **G** **D/F♯** **Em7** **G/A**   **D**

Fulness of God in   help-   less Babe!

       G   **D**   **G**   **A**

This gift of love and righteous-ness,

D/F♯   **G** **D/F♯** **Em7** **G/A**   **D**

Scorned by the ones He   came   to save;

     D/F♯ **G**   **D/F♯** **Asus** **A**

Till on that cross as Jesus   died,

      D/F♯ **G**   **Bm7** **Asus** **A**

The wrath of God was satis- fied–

     G   **D**   **G**   **A**

For every sin on Him was laid;

D/F♯   **G** **D/F♯** **Em7** **G/A** **D** **Dsus/A** **D**

Here in the death of   Christ   I live.

Additional Verses:

Verse 3   There in the ground His body lay,
Light of the world by darkness slain:
Then bursting forth in glorious day
Up from the grave He rose again!
And as He stands in victory
Sin's curse has lost its grip on me,
For I am His and He is mine–
Bought with the precious blood of Christ.

Verse 4   No guilt in life, no fear in death,
This is the pow'r of Christ in me;
From life's first cry to final breath,
Jesus commands my destiny.
No pow'r of hell, no scheme of man,
Can ever pluck me from His hand;
Till He returns or calls me home,
Here in the pow'r of Christ I'll stand.

In the Secret
(I Want to Know You)

Words and Music by
ANDY PARK

Melody:

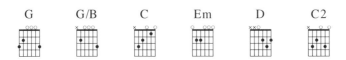

In the se - cret, in the qui - et place, ___

G   G/B   C   Em   D   C2

Verse 1

G   G/B   C
In the secret,   in the quiet place,
Em   D   C2
In the stillness, You are there.
G   G/B   C
In the secret,   in the quiet hour I wait only for You,
Em   D   C2
'Cause I want to know You more.

Chorus

G   D   Em   C2
I want to know You,   I want to hear Your voice,
G   D   C   G/B   C
I want to know You more.
G   D   Em   C2
I want to touch You,   I want to see Your face,
G   D   C   G/B   C
I want to know You more.

Verse 2   **G**   **G/B**   **C**

             I am reaching   for the highest goal,

       Em   **D**   **C2**

            That I might receive the prize.

       G   **G/B**

          Pressing onward,

                   C

Pushing every hindrance aside, out of my way,

       Em   **D**   **C2**

           'Cause I want to know You more.

Indescribable

Words and Music by
JESSE REEVES
and LAURA STORY

Melody:

From the high - est of heights

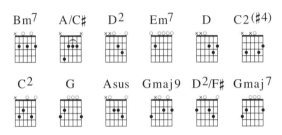

Verse 1

Bm7   **A/C♯**   **D2**
   From the highest of heights to the depths of the sea,
Em7   **D**   **C2(♯4)**
   Creation's revealing Your majesty.
Bm7   **A/C♯**   **D2**
   From the colors of fall to the fragrance of spring,
Em7   **D**   **C2**
   Every creature's unique in a song that it sings.
G   **Asus**
All exclaiming:

Chorus   **D2**   **Asus**
           Indescribable,   uncontainable,
           Gmaj9
           You placed the stars in the sky,
                                  Bm7
           And You know them by name.
           D2/F♯   **Gmaj9**
           You are amazing God.
           D2   **Asus**
             All powerful,   untamable,
           Gmaj9   **Bm7**
           Awestruck, we fall to our knees, and we humbly proclaim
              D2/F♯   **Gmaj9**
           That You are amazing God.

Verse 2 **Bm7**   **A/C♯**   **D2**
             Who has told every lightning bolt where it should go,
           Em7   **D**   **C2(♯4)**
             Or seen heavenly storehouses laden with snow?
           Bm7   **A/C♯**   **D2**
             Who imagined the sun and gives source to its light,
           Em7   **D**   **C2**
             Yet conceals it to bring us the coolness of night?
           G   **Asus**
           None can fathom.

Bridge   **Bm7** **D2/F♯**   **Em7** **Bm7**
             You are amazing God.
           D2/F♯   **Gmaj7**
           You are amazing God.

Alt. Chorus **D2**   **Asus**
             Incomparable,   unchangeable,
           Gmaj9   **Bm7**
           You see the depths of my heart, and You love me the same.
           D2/F♯   **Gmaj9**
           You are amazing God.

Jesus, Messiah

Words and Music by
CHRIS TOMLIN, DANIEL CARSON,
ED CASH and JESSE REEVES

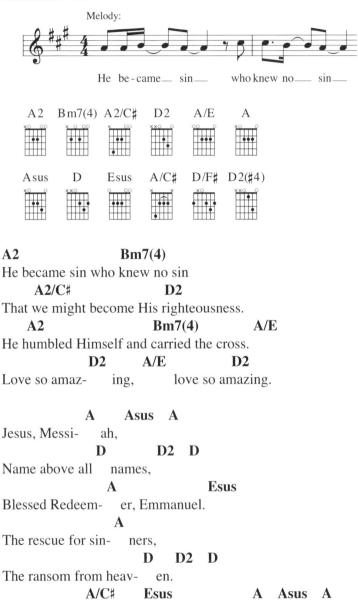

Melody:

He be-came— sin— who knew no— sin—

Verse 1

A2   Bm7(4)
He became sin who knew no sin
    A2/C♯   D2
That we might become His righteousness.
    A2   Bm7(4)   A/E
He humbled Himself and carried the cross.
               D2   A/E   D2
Love so amaz-   ing,   love so amazing.

Chorus

                    A   Asus   A
Jesus, Messi-   ah,
                 D   D2   D
Name above all   names,
                   A   Esus
Blessed Redeem-   er, Emmanuel.
                   A
The rescue for sin-   ners,
                 D   D2   D
The ransom from heav- en.
             A/C♯   Esus   A   Asus   A
Jesus, Messi-   ah,   Lord of all.

Verse 2   **A2**   **Bm7(4)**

His body, the bread; His blood, the wine,

A2/C♯   **D2**

Broken and poured out all for love.

      A2   **Bm7(4)**   **A/E**

The whole earth trembled, and the veil was torn.

          D2   **A/E**   **D2**

Love so amaz-   ing,   love so amazing, yeah!

Bridge   **Bm7(4)**   **A2/C♯**

All our hope   is in You.

          D2   **Esus**

All our hope   is in You.

        Bm7(4)   **A2/C♯**   **D2**

All the glo-   ry to You,   God.

        Esus

The light of the world!

Tag   **D/F♯**   **A/E**   **Esus**   **D** **D2(♯4)** **D2**

Jesus, Messi-   ah,   Lord of all!

        D **D2(♯4)** **D2**   **D** **D2(♯4)** **D**

Lord of all!   Lord of all!

      A

Lord of all!

Let Everything That Has Breath

Words and Music by
MATT REDMAN

Melody:

Let ev - 'ry - thing that,

| E | E/D♯ | C♯m7 | A2 | A2/B | F♯m7 | B |

Chorus

E   **E/D♯**
   Let everything that,   everything that,
C♯m7   **A2**   **A2/B**
   Everything that has breath praise the Lord.
E   **E/D♯**
   Let everything that,   everything that,
C♯m7   **A2**   **A2/B**
   Everything that has breath praise the Lord.

Verse 1

E   **E/D♯**
   Praise You in the morning,   praise You in the evening,
C♯m7   **A2**
   Praise You when I'm young and when I'm old.
E
   Praise You when I'm laughing,
E/D♯
   Praise You when I'm grieving,
C♯m7   **A2**
   Praise You every season of the soul.

GUITAR CHORD SONGBOOK

Pre-   **F♯m7**   **A2/B**
Chorus

If we (they) could see how much You're worth,

       F♯m7   **A2/B**

Your pow'r, Your might, Your endless love,

       F♯m7   **A2/B**   **A2**   **B**

Then surely we (they) would never cease to praise.

Verse 2   **E**   **E/D♯**

       Praise You in the heavens,   joining with the angels,

    C♯m7   **A2**

       Praising You forever and a day.

    E   **E/D♯**

       Praise You on the earth now,   joining with creation,

    C♯m7   **A2**

       Calling all the nations to Your praise.

Let the Praises Ring

Words and Music by
LINCOLN BREWSTER

Melody:

Oh Lord, — my God, — in You I put — my trust.

C	F/C	Csus	G/B	Am	F

C2	Am7	G(add4)	F2	G	G/C

Verse 1

        C   **F/C**   **C**   **F/C**
Oh Lord, my God, in You I put my trust.
        C   **F/C**   **C**   **F/C**
Oh Lord, my God, in You I put my hope.
        C   **F/C**   **C**   **F/C**
Oh Lord, my God, in You I put my trust.
        C   **F/C**   **C**   **Csus**   **C**
Oh Lord, my God, in You I put my hope.

Chorus   **G/B**   **Am**
In   You,
   F   **C**   **C2** **Csus** **C**
In You I find my peace.
G/B   **Am**
In   You,
   F   **C**   **C2** **Csus** **C**
In You I find my strength.
G/B   **Am**
In   You,
   F   **C**   **C2** **Csus** **C**
I live and move and breathe.
G/B   **Am7**
    Let everything I say and do
   G(add4)
Be founded by my faith in You.
 F2   **G**
I lift up holy hands and say,
               C **G/C** **F2** **C** **G/C** **F2**
"Let the praises ring!"

Verse 2   **C**   **F/C**   **C**   **F/C**
Oh Lord, my God, to You I give my hands.
       C   **F/C**   **C** **F/C**
Oh Lord, my God, to You I give my feet.
       C   **F/C**   **C** **F/C**
Oh Lord, my God, to You I give my everything.
      C   **F/C**   **C** **Csus** **C**
Take all I am – to You I give my life.

Tag   **C** **G/C** **F2**   **C**
                   Let the praises ring!

Lord, Reign in Me

Words and Music by
BRENTON BROWN

Melody:

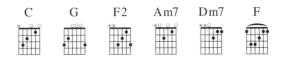

O-ver all the— earth— You— reign on—high,

C	G	F2	Am7	Dm7	F

Verse 1

    C   **G**   **F2**   **G**
Over all the earth You reign on high,

    C   **G**   **F2**   **G**
Every mountain stream, every sunset sky.

   Am7   **G**   **F2**   **G** **Dm7**
But my one request, Lord, my only aim

             F   **G**
Is that You'd reign in me again.

Chorus

    C   **G**   **F**   **G**
Lord, reign in me, reign in Your power,

    C   **G**   **F**   **G**
Over all my dreams, in my darkest hour;

  Am7   **G**   **F**   **G** **Dm7**
You are the Lord of all I am.

          F   **G** **C** **G** **F2** **C** **G** **F2**
So won't You reign in me again?

Verse 2   **C**   **G**   **F2**   **G**

          Over every thought, over every word,

          C   **G**   **F2**   **G**

          May my life reflect the beauty of my Lord.

          Am7   **G**   **F2**

           'Cause You mean more to me

             G   **Dm7**

          Than any earthly thing.

                 F   **G**

          So won't You reign in me again?

Tag   **F**   **G**   **Dm7**

          So won't You reign in me again?

             F   **G**   **Dm7**

          Won't You reign in me again?

             F   **G**   **C**

          Won't You reign in me again?

Love the Lord

Words and Music by
LINCOLN BREWSTER

Melody:

Love the Lord— Your God— with all—your heart,—

G   D   Em   Bm7   C   C2   D2/F♯   Em7

Verse 1

    G   **D**
Love the Lord Your God
             Em   **Bm7**
With all your heart, with all your soul,
             C   **D G**   **D C D**
With all your mind and with all your strength.
(repeat)
             C2   **D**
With all your heart, with all your soul,
             Em7   **D2/F♯**
With all your mind, with all your strength.
G   **D**
Love the Lord Your God
             Em   **Bm7**
With all your heart, with all your soul,
             C   **D G**   **D C D**
With all your mind and with all your strength.

Verse 2   **G**   **D**
             I will serve You, Lord,
                     Em   **Bm7**
             With all my heart, with all my soul,
                  C   **D G**   **D C D**
             With all my mind and with all my strength.
             (repeat)
                 C2   **D**
             With all my heart, with all my soul,
                 Em7   **D2/F♯**
             With all my mind, with all my strength.
             G   **D**
             I will serve You, Lord,
                     Em   **Bm7**
             With all my heart, with all my soul,
                  C   **D G**   **D C D**
             With all my mind and with all my strength.

Bridge   **G**   **C2**
             I will love You. (I will love You.)
             Em7   **C2**
             I will praise You. (I will praise You.)
             G   **C2**
             I will serve You. (I will serve You.)
             Em7   **C2**   **D**
             I will trust You. (I will trust You.)

Let God Arise

Words and Music by
CHRIS TOMLIN, ED CASH
and JESSE REEVES

Melody:

Hear the ho - ly roar of God___ re-sound.___

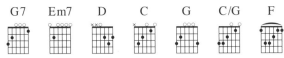

G7   Em7   D   C   G   C/G   F

Verse 1

           G7
Hear the holy roar of God resound.

Watch the waters part before us now.
         Em7
Come and see what He has done for us.
D
Tell the world of His great love.

**Pre-
Chorus**

     C   **Em7**   **D**   **C**   **Em7**   **D**
Our God is a God who saves. Our God is a God who saves.

       G   **C/G**
Let God arise. Let God arise.
       G7   **C/G**

Chorus   Our God reigns now and forever. He reigns now and forever.

Interlude   F G7 C F G7 C

Verse 2

         G7
His enemies will run for sure.

The church will stand; she will endure.
     Em7
He holds the keys of life, our Lord.
     D
Death has no sting, no final words.

Made Me Glad

Words and Music by
MIRIAM WEBSTER

Melody:

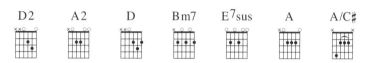

I will— bless the Lord for - ev - er.——

Capo 1st fret and play in A

| D2 | A2 | D | Bm7 | E7sus | A | A/C♯ |

Verse 1

> **D2**   **A2   D2**   **A2**
> I will bless the Lord forever. I will trust Him at all times.
> **D2**   **A2**
> He has delivered me from all fear.
> **D2**   **A2**
> He has set my feet upon a rock.
>   **D**   **Bm7**   **E7sus**
> And I will not be moved, and I'll say of the Lord,

Chorus

>   **A**   **Bm7**   **D**   **E7sus**
> You are my shield, my strength, my portion, Deliverer;
>   **A**   **A/C♯**
> My shelter, strong tower;
>   **D**   **E7sus**   **D2**   (**A** - *last time*)
> My very present help in time of need.

Verse 2

> **D2**   **A2   D2**   **A2**
> I will bless the Lord forever. I will trust Him at all times.
> **D2**   **A2**
> Whom have I in heaven but You?
> **D2**   **A2**
> There's none I desire besides You.
>   **D**   **Bm7**   **E7sus**
> And You have made me glad, and I'll say of the Lord,

Made to Worship

Words and Music by
CHRIS TOMLIN, ED CASH
and STEPHAN SHARP

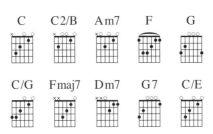

Be - fore the day, —   be - fore the light, —

Verse 1
    C   **C2/B**
Before the day, before the light,
    Am7   **F**
Before the world revolved around the sun,
    C   **C2/B**
God on high stepped down into time
                  Am7   **F** **G**
And wrote the story of His love for everyone.

Pre-   **F**   **G**
Chorus   He has filled our hearts with wonder
    F   **C/G**   **F**
So that we always remember:

Chorus   **C**
              You and I are made to worship;
              Fmaj7
              You and I are called to love.
              Dm7   **G7**
              You and I are forgiven and free.
                    C
              When you and I embrace surrender,
                    Fmaj7
              When you and I choose to believe,
                  Dm7   **G7**   **C**
              Then you and I will see who we were meant to be.

Verse 2   **C**   **C2/B**
              All we are and all we have
                 Am7   **F**
              Is all a gift from God that we receive.
              C   **C2/B**
              Brought to life, we open up our eyes
                          Am7   **F**   **G**
              To see the majesty and glory of the King.

Bridge   **Dm7**   **C/E**
                    Even the rocks cry out,
                          F
              Even the heavens shout
                          G7
              At the sound of His holy name.
              Dm7   **C/E**
                    So let every voice sing out;
                          F
              Let every knee bow down.
                          G7
              He's worthy of all our praise.

Majesty
(Here I Am)

Words and Music by
MARTIN SMITH
and STUART GARRARD

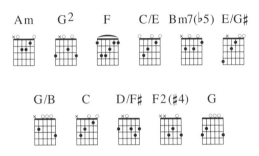

Verse 1

Am G2 F C/E   F
Here I   am, humbled by Your Majesty,
C/E   Bm7(♭5) E/G♯
Covered by Your grace so free.
Am G2 F C/E   F
Here I   am, knowing I'm a sinful man,
C/E   Bm7(♭5) E/G♯
Covered by the blood of the Lamb.

**Pre-
Chorus**

Am G/B C
Now I've found
                              Am G/B C
The greatest love of all   is   mine
                              D/F♯
Since You laid down Your life,
                    F F2(♯4) F F2(♯4)
The greatest sacrifice.

Chorus 1

C   G   Am   F
Majesty,   Majesty,
        C   G
Your grace has found me just as I am,
        Am   F
Empty-handed but alive in Your hands.

Verse 2

Am   G2   F   C/E   F
Here   I   am, humbled by the love that You give,
   C/E   Bm7(♭5)   E/G♯
Forgiven so that I can forgive.
Am   G2   F   C/E   F
Here   I   stand, knowing that I'm Your desire,
C/E   Bm7(♭5)   E/G♯
Sanctified by glory and fire.

Chorus 2

            C   G   Am   F
Singing, Majesty,   Majesty,
        C   G
Forever I am changed by Your love
       Am   F
In the presence of Your Majesty,
       Am   G2   F
Majesty.

Marvelous Light

Words and Music by
CHARLIE HALL

In - to mar - vel - ous light I'm run - ning,

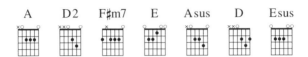

A   D2   F#m7   E   Asus   D   Esus

Chorus

A
   Into marvelous light I'm running,
D2
   Out of darkness, out of shame.
F#m7   **E**
   Through the cross, You are the Truth,
  D2   **A**   **(Asus)**
You are the Life, You are the Way.

Verse 1

A   **D2**
   I once was fatherless,   a stranger with no hope.
A
   Your kindness wakened me,
D2
Wakened me from my sleep now.
A   **D2**
   Your love, it beckons deeply,   a call to come and die.
A
   By grace, now I will come
   D2
And take this life, take Your life.

***Pre-
Chorus***

F#m7   **E**   **D2**
   Sin has lost its power;   death has lost its sting.
F#m7   **E**   **D**
   From the grave You've risen   victoriously.

Verse 2   **A**

        My dead heart now is beating,

    D2

        My deepest stains now clean.

    A

        Your breath fills up my lungs.

    D2

    Now, I'm free; now, I'm free.

    A

        My dead heart now is beating,

    D2

        My deepest stains now clean.

    A

        Your breath fills up my lungs.

    D2

    Now, I'm free; now, I'm free.

Channel   **D2**   **Asus** **F♯m7**   **Esus**
(spoken) *There's no more shame,   no more shame.*

    D2

        And now we show the world Christ in you.

Bridge   **A**

        Lift my hands and spin around,

    D2   **Esus**

        See the light that I have found.

    F♯m7   **Esus**

          Oh, the marvelous light,

    D2

    Marvelous light, it's Christ in you.

    A

        Lift my hands and spin around,

    D2   **Esus**

        See the light that I have found.

    F♯m7   **Esus**   **D2**

        Oh, the marvelous light, marvelous light.

Mighty to Save

Words and Music by
BEN FIELDING
and REUBEN MORGAN

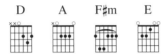

Verse 1

   D   **A**
Everyone needs compassion,
                 F♯m
Love that's never failing.
      E   **D**
Let mercy fall on me.
                       A
Everyone needs forgiveness,
               F♯m
The kindness of a Savior,
      E   **D** **E** **D** **E**
The hope of nations.

Chorus   **A**   **E**
            Savior, He can move the mountains.
                D   **A**
            My God is mighty to save.
             F♯m   **E**
            He is mighty to save.
            A   **E**
            Forever, Author of salvation.
                D   **A**
            He rose and conquered the grave.
            F♯m   **E**
            Jesus conquered the grave.

Verse 2   **D**   **A**
             So take me as You find me,
                 F♯m
            All my fears and failures.
            E   **D**
            Fill my life again.
                  A
            I give my life to follow,
                 F♯m
            Everything I believe in.
             E   **D** **E** **D** **E**
            Now, I surrender.

Bridge   **D**   **A**   **E**
            Shine your light and   let the whole world see.
             F♯m   **D**   **A**   **E**   **F♯m**
            We're singing   for the glory   of the risen King Jesus.
            D   **A**   **E**
            Shine your light and   let the whole world see.
             F♯m   **D**   **A**   **E**
            We're singing   for the glory of the risen King.

My Redeemer Lives

Words and Music by
REUBEN MORGAN

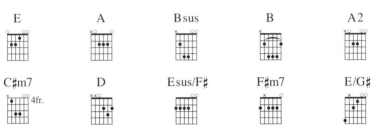

Verse

> E   A
> I know He rescued my soul,
>
> E   A
> His blood, has covered my sin,
>
>   E   A   E   A
> I believe,   I believe.
>
> E   A
> My shame, He's taken away,
>
> E   A
> My pain is healed in His name.
>
>   E   A   E   A
> I believe,   I believe.
>
> **Bsus**   **B**
> I'll raise a banner
>
> A   B
> 'Cause my Lord has conquered the grave!

© Copyright 1998 Reuben Morgan / Hillsong Publishing (ASCAP) (Administered in the U.S. and Canada by Integrity Worship Music). This arrangement © Copyright 2010 Reuben Morgan / Hillsong Publishing (ASCAP) (Administered in the U.S. and Canada by Integrity Worship Music) (c/o Integrity Media, Inc., 1000 Cody Road, Mobile, AL 36695). All rights reserved. International copyright secured. Used by permission.

Chorus   **E**   **A2**   **C♯m7** **B**
My Redeemer lives! My Redeemer lives!
                       E   **A2**   **C♯m7** **B**
My Redeemer lives! My Redeemer lives!

Bridge   **D**   **Esus/F♯**
You lift my burden,   and I rise with You.
              E   **F♯m7**   **E/G♯**   **B**
I'm dancing on this mountaintop to see Your kingdom come.

Majestic

Words and Music by
LINCOLN BREWSTER

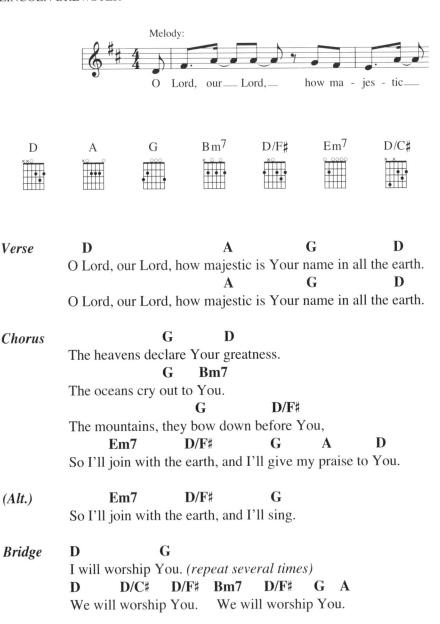

Verse
    D   A   G   D
O Lord, our Lord, how majestic is Your name in all the earth.
             A   G   D
O Lord, our Lord, how majestic is Your name in all the earth.

Chorus
        G   D
The heavens declare Your greatness.
        G   Bm7
The oceans cry out to You.
           G   D/F♯
The mountains, they bow down before You,
     Em7   D/F♯   G   A   D
So I'll join with the earth, and I'll give my praise to You.

(Alt.)
     Em7   D/F♯   G
So I'll join with the earth, and I'll sing.

Bridge
    D   G
I will worship You. *(repeat several times)*
    D   D/C♯ D/F♯ Bm7 D/F♯ G A
We will worship You.   We will worship You.

My Savior Lives

Words and Music by
JON EGAN and
GLENN PACKIAM

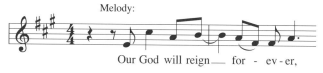

Melody:

Our God will reign — for - ev - er,

A   F#m7   D   Bm7   G2

Verse 1

A   F#m7   D
Our God will reign forever,
A   F#m7   D
And all the world will know His name.
A   F#m7   D   A   F#m7   D   Bm7
Everyone   together,   sing the song of the redeemed.

Chorus

A
I know that my Redeemer lives,
F#m7
     And now I stand on what He did.
D   A
My Savior, my Savior lives.

Every day a brand new chance to say,
F#m7
     "Jesus, You are the only Way."
D   A
My Savior, my Savior lives.

Verse 2

A   F#m7   D
The King has come from heaven
A   F#m7   D
And darkness trembles at His name.
A   F#m7   D   A   F#m7   D   Bm7
Victory   forever   is the song of the redeemed.

Tag

A   F#m7   G2   Bm7
My Savior lives. My Savior lives. My Savior lives.

My Savior, My God

Words and Music by
AARON SHUST
and DOROTHY GREENWELL

Melody:

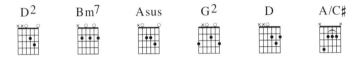

I am not skilled to un-der-stand

D2   Bm7   Asus   G2   D   A/C♯

Verse 1
                             D2
I am not skilled to understand
                                          Bm7
What God has willed, what God has planned.
                           Asus
I only know at His right hand
                         D2
Stands One who is my Savior.

Verse 2
                             D2
I take Him at His word and deed.
                                  Bm7
Christ died to save me, this I read.
                           Asus
And in my heart I find a need
                         D2
Of Him to be my Savior.

Pre-
Chorus

         G2
That He would leave His place on high
       D2
And come for sinful man to die,
          Asus
You count it strange; so once did I
      D2
Before I knew my Savior.

Chorus

    Bm7   **G2**
My Savior loves. My Savior lives.
     D   **Asus**
My Savior's always there for me.
    Bm7   **G2**
My God He was. My God He is.
     D   **Asus**
My God is always gonna be.

Verse 3

        D2
Yes, living, dying, let me bring
           Bm7
My strength, my solace from this spring:
         Asus
That He who lives to be my King
      D2
Once died to be my Savior.

Alt.
Chorus

    Bm7
My Savior loves. My Savior lives.
    A/C♯
My Savior's always there for me.
    G2
My God He was. My God He is.
      Asus
My God is always gonna be.

Not to Us

Words and Music by
CHRIS TOMLIN
and JESSE REEVES

Melody:

The cross— be - fore— me, the world— be - hind,—

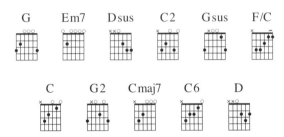

G   Em7   Dsus   C2   Gsus   F/C

C   G2   Cmaj7   C6   D

Verse 1

G   Em7
  The cross before me, the world behind,

  No turning back; raise the banner high.
Dsus   **C2**   **G Gsus G**
  It's not for me; it's all for You.

  Let the heavens shake and split the sky.
Em7
  Let the people clap their hands and cry.
Dsus   **C2**   **G Gsus G**
  It's not for us;   it's all for You.

Chorus

G   F/C   C   F/C   C
Not to us, but to Your name   be the glory.
G   F/C   C   F/C   C
Not to us, but to Your name   be the glory.

Interlude   G G2 **Cmaj7** C F/C C

Verse 2   **G**   **Em7**
          Our hearts unfold before Your throne,

       The only place for those who know.
Dsus   **C2**   **G** **Gsus** **G**
        It's not for us; it's all for You.

       Send Your holy fire on this offering.
Em7
         Let our worship burn for the world to see.
Dsus   **C2**   **G** **Gsus** **G**
        It's not for us;   it's all for You.

Bridge 1   **G**
       The earth is shaking, the mountains shouting;
C6 **C**   **C6** **C**
       It's all for You.
     Em7   **Dsus**   **C**
       The waves are crashing; the sun is raging.   It's all for You.
     G   **C6** **C**   **C6** **C**
       The universe spinning and singing;   it's all for You.
     Em7   **Dsus**   **C**
       Your children dancing, dancing, dancing;   it's all for You.
          Gsus **G** **Gsus** **G** **C2** **C** **Cmaj7** **C**
       It's all for You.

Bridge 2   **G**
       All glory and honor and praise,
       Cmaj7
       All glory and honor and praise,
       Em7   **D**
       All glory and honor and praise,
       Cmaj7
       All glory and honor and praise.

Tag   **G**   **F/C** **C**   **F/C** **C**
       Not to us, but to Your name   be the glory.
       Em7   **D**   **C**   **G**
       Not to us,   but to Your name.

O Praise Him
(All This for a King)

Words and Music by
DAVID CROWDER

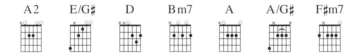

A2	E/G♯	D	Bm7	A	A/G♯	F♯m7

Verse 1

    A2   **E/G♯**   **D**
Turn your ear to heaven and hear the noise inside,
    A2
The sound of angel's awe,
    E/G♯   **D**
The sound of angel's songs, and all this for a King.
Bm7   **D**
We could join and sing all to Christ the King.

Pre-
Chorus 1

E/G♯   **D**
    How constant, how   divine,
E/G♯   **D**
    This song of ours   will rise.
E/G♯   **D**
O how constant, how   divine,
E/G♯   **D**
    This love of ours   will rise, will rise.

Chorus 1   **A**   **A/G♯**
O praise Him, O praise Him;
F♯m7   **D**   **Bm7**   **A**
He is holy, He is ho-   ly, yeah.

Verse 2   **A2**   **E/G♯**   **D**
Turn your gaze to heaven and raise a joyous noise,
     A2
The sound of salvation come,
     E/G♯   **D**
The sound of rescued ones, and all this for a King.
Bm7   **D**
Angels join to sing all for Christ the King.

Pre-   **E/G♯**   **D**
Chorus 2   How infinite   and sweet,
     E/G♯   **D**
This love so res-   cuing.
     E/G♯   **D**
O how infinite-   ly sweet,
     E/G♯   **D**
This great love that has   redeemed. As one we sing.

Chorus 2   **A**   **A/G♯**
Alleluia! Alleluia!
F♯m7   **D**   **Bm7**   **A**
He is holy, He is ho-   ly, yeah.

Once Again

Words and Music by
MATT REDMAN

Melody:

Je-sus Christ,— I think up-on Your sac-ri-fice;

| D | A/D | G/D | G | D/F♯ | Asus |
| A | D2 | Dsus | G2 | Bm | G/B |

Verse 1

  D   A/D   G/D   D
Jesus Christ, I think upon Your sacrifice;
  G   D/F♯   G   Asus   A
You became nothing, poured out to death.
  D   A/D   G/D   D
Many times I've wondered at Your gift of life,
    G   Asus   A   D   D2   D
And I'm in that place once a-   gain.
  G   Asus   A   D   Dsus
I'm in that place once a-   gain.

Chorus

  D/F♯   G2   D/F♯   Asus   A
Once again I look upon the cross where You died.
    D/F♯   G2   D/F♯   Asus   A
I'm humbled by Your mercy, and I'm broken inside.
  Bm   G
Once again I thank You,
  D/F♯   A   G/B Asus   A   D
Once again I pour out my life.

Verse 2   **D**   **A/D   G/D**   **D**
Now You are exalted to the highest place,
G   **D/F♯**   **G**   **Asus**   **A**
King of the heavens, where one day I'll bow.
D   **A/D   G/D**   **D**
But, for now, I marvel at this saving grace,
      G   **Asus**   **A   D   D2   D**
And I'm full of praise once a-   gain.
G   **Asus**   **A   D   Dsus**
I'm full of praise once a-   gain.

Bridge   **G**   **Asus**   **A**   **D/F♯**
Thank You for the cross,   Thank You for the cross,
G   **Asus**   **A   D**
Thank You for the cross,   my Friend.

One Way

Words and Music by
JOEL HOUSTON
and JONATHON DOUGLASS

Melody:

I lay my life down at Your feet.

Capo 2nd fret and play in A

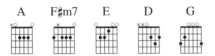

A   F♯m7   E   D   G

Verse 1   **A**

I lay my life down at Your feet.

F♯m7

You're the only One I need.

E   **D**

I turn to You, and You are always there.

A

In troubled times, it's You I seek.

F♯m7

I put You first; that's all I need.

E   **D**

I humble all I am, all to You.

Chorus   **A**   **E**
One way,   Jesus,
F♯m7   **D**
You're the only One that I could live for.
A   **E**
One way,   Jesus,
F♯m7   **G**
You're the only One that I could live for.

Verse 2   **A**
You are always, always there,
F♯m7
Every how and everywhere.
E   **D**
Your grace abounds so deeply within me.
A
You will never, ever change:
F♯m7
Yesterday, today the same.
E   **D**
Forever 'til forever meets no end.

Bridge   **A**   **E**
You are the Way, the Truth, and the Life.
   F♯m7   **D**   **F♯m7**
We live by faith and not by sight for You.
      E   **D**
We're living all for You.

Offering

Words and Music by
PAUL BALOCHE

Melody:

The sun— can-not— com-pare—

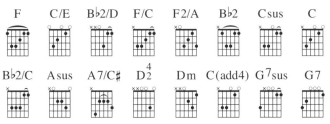

Verse

    F   C/E   Bb2/D   F/C
The sun cannot compare to the glory of Your love;
F2/A   **Bb2**   **Csus**   **C** **Bb2/C**
There is no shadow in Your presence;
    F   C/E   Bb2/D   F/C
No mortal man would dare to stand before Your throne,
F2/A   **Bb2**   **Csus**   **C**
Before the Holy One of heaven;
    Bb2/D   **C/E**   **F**
It's only   by Your blood,
         Asus   **A7/C#**   **D4(2)**   **Dm**
And it's only   through Your mer-   cy,
C   **Bb2**   **F**
Lord, I   come.

Chorus

    F2/A   **Bb2**   **Csus**   **F**
I bring an offering of worship to my King;
    F2/A   **Bb2**   **Csus**   **F**
No one on earth deserves the praises that I sing;
    F2/A   **Bb2**
Jesus, may You receive
    C(add4)   **G7sus** **G7**
The honor that You're due;
    Bb2   **Csus**   **F**
O Lord, I bring an offering to You.
    C/E **F** **Bb2/D**   **Bb2**   **F**
I bring an offering to You.

Open the Eyes of My Heart

Words and Music by
PAUL BALOCHE

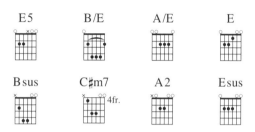

O - pen the eyes— of my heart, —Lord;

Chorus

E5   **B/E**
Open the eyes of my heart, Lord; open the eyes of my heart.

       A/E   **E**
I want to see You, I want to see You.

Verse

          Bsus   **C♯m7**
To see You high and lifted up,

A2   **Bsus**
Shining in the light of Your glory.

            C♯m7   **A2**   **Bsus**
Pour out Your pow'r and love as we sing holy, holy, holy.

Bridge

E5   **B/E**
Holy, holy, holy. Holy, holy, holy.

A/E   **E**   **Esus**
Holy, holy, holy. I want to see You.

Tag

      E   **Esus**   **E**
I want to see You.   I want to see You.

Our God Saves

Words and Music by
PAUL BALOCHE
and BRENTON BROWN

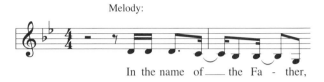

Melody:

In the name of ___ the Fa - ther,

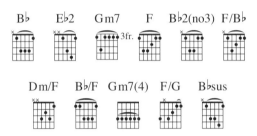

Verse

           Bb
In the name of the Father, in the name of the Son,
           Eb2
In the name of the Spirit, Lord, we come.
           Gm7
We're gathered together to lift up Your name,
           Eb2
To call on our Savior, to fall on Your grace.

Channel

           Bb
Hear the joyful sounds of our offering
           F
As Your saints bow down, as Your people sing.
           Gm7
We will rise with You, lifted on Your wings,
           Eb2
And the world will see that

Chorus   **B♭   B♭2(no3)   B♭   B♭2(no3)**
Our God saves.
F/B♭   B♭   F   Dm/F   F
Our   God saves.
       B♭/F   Gm7   Gm7(4)   Gm7   Gm7(4)
There is   hope
F/G   Gm7   E♭2
In   Your   name.
         B♭   B♭2(no3)   B♭   B♭2(no3)
Mourning turns
   F/B♭   B♭   F   Dm/F   F
To songs   of   praise.
     B♭/F   Gm7   Gm7(4)   Gm7   Gm7(4)
Our God   saves.
F/G   Gm7   E♭2
Our   God   saves.

Tag   **B♭   B♭sus   B♭   B♭2(no3)**
Our God saves.   Our God saves.
         B♭   B♭sus   B♭
Our God saves.   Our God saves.

Our Great God

Words and Music by
MAC POWELL
and FERNANDO ORTEGA

Melody:

E - ter - nal— God, un - chang - ing,

C   Gm7   Am   F   Dm   E/G♯   D/F♯   Dm7   G

Verse 1

      C   Gm7   C
Eternal God, unchanging, mysterious, and unknown,
      C   Gm7   C
Your boundless love, unfailing in grace and mercy shown.
           Am   F
Bright seraphim in ceaseless flight
       Am   F
Around Your glorious throne,
        C   Gm7   C
They raise their voices day and night in praise to You alone.

Chorus

     C Gm7   F   C
Hallelu- jah! Glory be to our great God.
     C Gm7   F   C
Hallelu- jah! Glory be to our great God.

Verse 2   **C**   **Gm7**   **C**
Lord, we are weak and frail, helpless in the storm.
        C   **Gm7**   **C**
Surround us with Your angels; hold us in Your arms.
    Am   **F**   **Am**   **F**
Our cold and ruthless enemy, his pleasure is our harm.
        C   **Gm7**   **C**
Rise up, O Lord, and he will flee before our sovereign God.

Interlude   **Dm** **F** **Am** **E/G♯** **D/F♯** **F** **Dm7** **G**

Verse 3   **C**   **Gm7**   **C**
Let every creature in the sea and every flying bird,
        C   **Gm7**   **C**
Let every mountain, every field and valley of the earth,
    Am   **F**   **Am**   **F**
Let all the moons and all the stars in all the universe
        C   **Gm7**   **C**
Sing praises to the living God, who rules them by His word.

Revelation Song

Words and Music by
JENNIE LEE RIDDLE

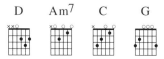

Verse 1

D   **Am7**
Worthy is the   Lamb who was slain.
C   **G**
Holy, holy is He.
D   **Am7**
Sing a new song   to Him who sits on
C   **G**
Heaven's mercy seat.

Chorus

D   **Am7**
Holy, Holy, Holy   is the Lord, God Almighty
C   **G**
Who was and is and is to come.
D
With all creation, I sing,
Am7
    "Praise to the King of kings!"
C   **G**
You are my everything, and I will adore You.

Verse 2   **D**   **Am7**
Clothed in rainbows   of living color,
C   **G**
Flashes of lightning, rolls of thunder.
D
Blessing and honor, strength and
Am7
Glory and power be
C   **G**
To You, the only wise King.

Verse 3   **D**   **Am7**
I'm filled with wonder,   awestruck wonder
C   **G**
At the mention of Your name.
D   **Am7**
Jesus, Your name is power,   breath and Living Water,
C   **G**
Such a marvelous mystery.

Salvation Is Here

Words and Music by
JOEL HOUSTON

God a - bove all the world in___ mo - tion.

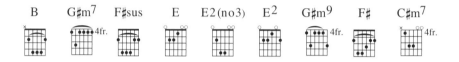

Verse 1   B   G#m7   F#sus   E   B
        God above all the world in motion.
        G#m7   **F#sus**   **E2(no3)**
        God above all my hopes and fears.
        B   **G#m7**   **F#sus**   **E2 G#m9**
        And I don't care what the world throws at me now,
        E
        It's gonna be alright.

Verse 2   B   G#m7   F#sus   E   B
        Hear the sound of the gener-   ations,
        G#m7   **F#sus**   **E2(no3)**
        Making loud our freedom song.
        B   **G#m7**   **F#sus**   **E2**   **G#m9**
        All in all that the world would know Your name.
        E
        It's gonna be alright.

Pre-
Chorus

        B   **E**
'Cause I know my God saved the day.
       F♯   **G♯m7**
And I know His Word never fails.
       B   **E**   **C♯m7**   **E**
And I know my God made a way for me.
          B
Salvation is   here.

Chorus

        G♯m7 **B**   **E**   **C♯m7**
Salvation is here.   Salvation is here, and He lives in me.
        G♯m7 **B**   **E**   **C♯m7**
Salvation is here.   Salvation that died just to set me free.
        G♯m7 **B**   **E**   **C♯m7**
Salvation is here.   Salvation is here, and He lives in me.
        G♯m7 **B**   **E**
Salvation is here   'cause You are alive,
           C♯m7
And You live in me.

Tag

        B   **E**   **F♯**
Salvation is here.   Salvation is here,
          G♯m7
And He lives in me.
        B   **E**   **F♯**
Salvation is here   'cause You are alive,
          G♯m7
And You live in me.

Shout to the Lord

Words and Music by
DARLENE ZSCHECH

Melody:

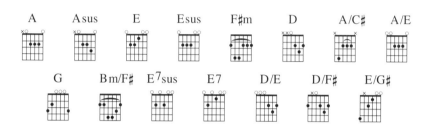

My Je - sus,   my Sav - ior,

A   Asus   E   Esus   F♯m   D   A/C♯   A/E

G   Bm/F♯   E⁷sus   E7   D/E   D/F♯   E/G♯

Verse

| A | Asus | A | E | Esus | E |

My Je-   sus,   my Sav-   ior,

F♯m   **E**   **D**

Lord, there is none like You;

         A/C♯   **D**   **A/E**

All of my days,   I want to praise

       F♯m   **G**   **Bm/F♯**   **E7sus**   **E7**

The wonders of Your might-y   love.

A   **Asus**   **A**   **E**   **Esus**   **E**

My com-   fort,   my shel-   ter,

F♯m   **E**   **D**

Tower of refuge and strength;

         A/C♯   **D**   **A/E**

Let every breath, all that I am,

F♯m   **G**   **Bm/F♯**   **E7sus**   **E7**

Never cease to wor-ship   You!

Chorus A   F♯m   D   D/E   E

Shout to the Lord, all the earth, let us sing,

A   F♯m   D   E7sus   E7

Power and majesty, Praise to the King;

F♯m   E   D

Mountains bow down and the seas will roar

     E   D/F♯   E/G♯   E7

At the sound of Your name.

A   F♯m   D   D/E   E

I sing for joy at the work of Your hands;

   A   F♯m   D   E7sus   E7

Forever, I'll love You, forever, I'll stand!

F♯m   E   D   E   A

Nothing compares to the promise I have in   You.

Shout to the North

Words and Music by
MARTIN SMITH

Melody:

Men of   faith,   rise   up   and   sing

G	D	C	Em	G/B	Dsus

Verse 1

        G   D   C   G   D   C
Men of faith, rise up and sing of the great and glorious King.

        G   D   C
You are strong when you feel weak,

        G   D   C
In your broken-ness complete.

Chorus   G   C   D G   C   D
Shout to the north and the south; sing to the east and the west.

Em **G**   C   D C   D   G
Je-   sus is Savior to all, Lord of heaven and earth.

Verse 2

        G   D   C   G   D   C
Rise up, women of the truth, stand and sing to broken hearts

        G   D   C
Who can know the healing pow'r

        G   D   C
Of our awesome King of love.

Verse 3
                        G   **D**   **C**
Rise up, church with broken wings,
         G   **D**   **C**
Fill this place with songs again
           G   **D**   **C**
Of our God who reigns on high.
         G   **D**   **C**
By His grace again we'll fly.

Bridge   **Em**   **C**
We've been through fire, we've been through rain;
    Em   **C**
We've been refined by the pow'r of His name.
    Em   **C**
We've fallen deeper in love with You.
          G/B   **Dsus** **D**
You've burned the truth on our lips.

Tag   **C**   **D**   **G** **C**   **D**   **G**
Lord of heaven and earth, Lord of heaven and earth.

Sing to the King

Words and Music by
BILLY JAMES FOOTE

Melody:

Sing to the King

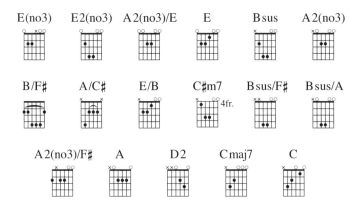

E(no3)   E2(no3)   A2(no3)/E   E   Bsus   A2(no3)

B/F♯   A/C♯   E/B   C♯m7   Bsus/F♯   Bsus/A

A2(no3)/F♯   A   D2   Cmaj7   C

Verse 1   **E(no3)   E2(no3)   A2(no3)/E   E**
        Sing to the King who is coming   to   reign.
        E(no3)   Bsus   A2(no3)   E
        Glory to Jesus, the Lamb that was slain.
                      B/F♯   A/C♯   E/B
        Life and salvation His empire shall bring,
        C♯m7   Bsus/F♯   Bsus/A   E(no3)
        Joy to the nations when Jesus is   King.

Chorus   **E**
Come, let us sing a song,
   A2(no3)/F♯   **A**
A song declaring we belong to Jesus.
        E   **D2** **A**
He's all we need.
E
Lift up a heart of praise.
A2(no3)/F♯   **A**
Sing now with voices raised to Jesus;
       E(no3)
Sing to the King.

Verse 2   **E(no3)**   **E2(no3)**   **A2(no3)/E**   **E**
For His returning we watch and we pray.
E(no3)   **Bsus**   **A2(no3)**   **E**
We will be ready the dawn of that day.
         B/F♯   **A/C♯** **E/B**
We'll join in singing with all the redeemed.
C♯m7 **Bsus/F♯**   **Bsus/A** **E(no3)**
Satan is vanquished, and Jesus is   King.

Bridge   **D2**   **A**   **E**
Sing to the King. Sing to   the King.
        Bsus   **D2** **A/C♯**   **Cmaj7**   **C**
Sing to the King.   Sing to the   King.

Sing, Sing, Sing

Words and Music by
CHRIS TOMLIN, DANIEL CARSON,
JESSE REEVES, MATT GILDER
and TRAVIS NUNN

Melody:

Sing, sing, sing, — and make mu - sic

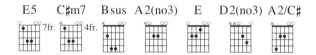

E5   C#m7   Bsus   A2(no3)   E   D2(no3)   A2/C#

Chorus

E5
We will sing, sing, sing and make music with the heavens.
C#m7
We will sing, sing, sing, grateful that You hear us
     Bsus   **A2(no3)**   **E5**
When we shout Your praise, lift high the name of Jesus.

Verse 1

E
What's not to love about You?
E
Heaven and earth adore You.
C#m7
Kings and kingdoms bow down.
C#m7   **Bsus**
Son of God, You are the One,
    A2(no3)   **E5**
You are the One   we're living for.

Verse 2   **E**
　　　　You are the love that frees us.
　　　　E　　　　　　　　　　　　**C#m7**
　　　　You are the light that leads us,　　like a fire burning.
C#m7　　　　　　　　　　　　**Bsus**
　　　　Son of God, You are the One,
　　　　　　　A2(no3)　　　　**E5**
You are the One　　　we're living for.

Tag　　　　**A2/C#**　　　**D2(no3)**　**A2(no3)**　**E**
Lift high the name of Jesus,　of　Jesus.

Sometimes by Step

Words and Music by
RICH MULLINS
and DAVID STRASSER

Melody:

Some - times the night___

G	D/G	C2/E	Dsus	D	Bm

C	Em	Am7	D/F#	C/E	D7sus

D7	C/G	Am	F	C2	G/D

Verse 1

G   D/G

Sometimes the night was beautiful,

G   D/G

Sometimes the sky was so far away,

C2/E   Dsus   D

Sometimes it seemed steep, so close you could touch it,

             Bm

But your heart would break.

           C   Bm

Sometimes the morning came too soon,

           C   Em

Sometimes the day could be so hot.

          Dsus   C

There was so much work left to do,

          Am7

But so much You'd already done.

Chorus

        G   D/F♯ D   C/E   D7sus D7 G
O God, You are my God,   and I will ever   praise You.

        G   D/F♯ D   C/E   D7sus D7 G
O God, You are my God,   and I will ever   praise You.

            Em   Dsus   D
I will seek You in the morning,

                 C   Am7
And I will learn to walk in Your ways;

          G   D/F♯   D
And step by step You'll lead me,

             C/E   D7sus D7 G (C/G D)
And I will follow You all of my   days.

Verse 2   G   D/G
Sometimes I think of Abraham,

        G   D/G   C2/E
How one star he saw had been lit for me.

                              Dsus   D   Bm
He was a stranger in this land, and I am that no less than he.

               C   Bm
And on this road to righteousness,

                 C   Em
Sometimes the climb can be so steep.

          Dsus   C   Am7
I may falter in my steps, but never beyond Your reach.

Tag   Em   Dsus   D
And I will follow You all of my days,

            Am   F C2
And I will follow You all of my days.

          G/D   D
And step by step You'll lead me,

             C/E   D7sus D7 G
And I will follow You all of my days.

Rescue

Words and Music by
JARED ANDERSON

Melody:

You are ____ the source ____ of life

Bm7   D/F#   G2   D2   D2/C#   Em7

Verse   **Bm7**   **D/F#** **G2**   **Bm7**   **D/F#**   **G2** **Bm7**
You are the source of life, and I can't be left behind.
          D/F#   **G2** **Bm7**   **D/F#**   **G2**
No one else will do,   and I will take hold of You.

Chorus   **D2**   **D2/C#**
'Cause I need you, Jesus, to come to my rescue.
Em7   **G2**
Where else can I go?
                   D2   **D2/C#**
There's no other name by which I am saved.
Em7   **G2**
Capture me with grace;
          Bm7 D/F# G2 Bm7 D/F# G2
I will follow You.

Bridge   **Bm7**   **D/F#**   **G2**   **Bm7**
I will follow You.   I will follow You.
                   D/F#   **G2**   **Bm7**
This world has nothing for me. I will follow You.

Tag   **Em7**   **G2**   **Em7**   **G2**
Capture me with grace. Capture me with grace.
          Bm7   **D/F#**   **G2**
I will follow You.
          Bm7   **D/F#**   **G2**
I will follow You.

Take My Life

(Holiness)

Words and Music by
SCOTT UNDERWOOD

Melody:

Ho - li - ness, —— ho - li - ness

E   A2   B   Bsus

Verse 1

E   A2   B   A2
    Holiness, holiness is what I long for;

E   A2   B   A2
    Holiness is what I need.

E   A2   B   A2   E A2 B A2
    Holiness, holiness is what You want from me.

Verse 2

E   A2   B   A2
    Faithfulness, faithfulness is what I long for;

E   A2   B   A2
    Faithfulness is what I need.

E   A2   B
    Faithfulness, faithfulness

A2   E A2 B Bsus
Is what You want from me.

Chorus

B   E A2   B   A2
    Take my heart   and form it;

E   A2   B   A2
    Take my mind;   transform it;

E A2   B   A2   E   A2   B A2
    Take my will;   conform it   To Yours, to Yours, O Lord.

Tag

E   A2   B
    To Yours, to Yours, O Lord.

Additional verses: Righteousness ... Purity ... etc.

That's Why We Praise Him

Words and Music by
TOMMY WALKER

Melody:

He came to— live,   live a   per - fect   life;

| C | G | F | G/F | Dm |

| C/E | Dm/F | Gsus | Am | G/B |

Verse 1

              C G   F
He came to live,   live a perfect life;

            C G   F
He came to be   the Living Word, our light.

            C G   F
He came to die   so we'd be reconciled;

            C G   F   G/F F G
He came to rise   to show His pow'r and   might.

Chorus

  C   G   F
That's why we praise Him, that's why we sing;

  C   G   F G/F F G
That's why we offer Him our ev-'ry-   thing.

  C   G   F
That's why we bow down and worship this King,

          Dm C/E Dm/F Gsus   Am
'Cause He gave His   ev-   'rything,

          Dm C/E Dm/F Gsus   C
'Cause He gave His   ev-   'rything.

Verse 2

	C	G	F
He came to live,   live again in us;

	C	G		F
He came to be   our conqu'ring King and Friend.

	C	G		F
He came to heal   and show the lost ones His love;

| | C | G | | F | G/F | F | G |
He came to go   prepare a place for   us.

Bridge   C   G/B   F   G   C   G/B   F   G
       Halle,   hallelujah.   Halle,   hallelujah.

The Heart of Worship

Words and Music by
MATT REDMAN

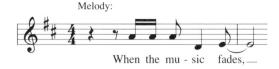

Melody:

When the mu - sic fades, —

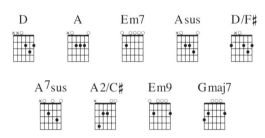

D   A   Em7   Asus   D/F♯

A7sus   A2/C♯   Em9   Gmaj7

Verse 1

D	A	Em7

When the music fades, all is stripped away,

Asus   A

And I simply come;

D   A   Em7

Longing just to bring something that's of worth

Asus   A

That will bless Your heart.

Pre-Chorus

Em7   D/F♯   A7sus

I'll bring You more than a song, for a song in itself

Em7   D/F♯   A7sus

Is not what You have required.

Em7   D/F♯   A7sus

You search much deeper within

Through the way things appear;

Em7   D/F♯   Asus   A

You're looking into my heart.

Chorus   **D**   **A2/C♯**

I'm coming back to the heart of worship,

   Em9   **D/F♯**   **Gmaj7**   **A7sus**

It's all about You, it's all about You, Jesus.

D   **A2/C♯**

I'm sorry, Lord, for the thing I've made it,

     Em9   **D/F♯**   **Gmaj7**   **A7sus**   **D**

When it's all about You,   all about You,   Jesus.

Verse 2   **D**   **A**   **Em7**

King of endless worth, no one could express

                   Asus   **A**

How much You deserve.

D   **A**   **Em7**

Though I'm weak and poor, all I have is Yours,

                 Asus   **A**

Every single breath.

The Potter's Hand

Words and Music by
DARLENE ZSCHECH

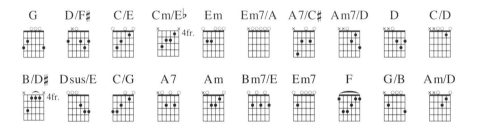

Verse 1

G   D/F♯
Beautiful Lord, wonderful Savior,
C/E   Cm/E♭
I know for sure all of my days are
Em   Em7/A A7/C♯ Am7/D D C/D
Held in Your hand, Crafted into Your perfect   plan.

Verse 2

G   D/F♯
You gently call me into Your presence
C/E   Cm/E♭
Guiding me by Your Holy Spirit.
Em
Teach me, dear Lord,
          Em7/A A7/C♯ Am7/D   D B/D♯
To live all of my life   through Your eyes.

Pre-
Chorus

Em   **D**   **Dsus/E** **D/F♯**
I'm captured by Your holy call-   ing,

G   **C/G**   **G**   **D/F♯** **Em**
Set me apart, I know You're draw-ing   me to Yourself;

Em7/A **A7**   **Am7/D** **D**
Lead me, Lord, I pray.

Chorus

G   **D/F♯**   **Am**   **Bm7/E** **Em7**
Take me, mold me, use me, fill   me;

 F   **C/E** **Am** **G/B** **Am** **Am7/D** **D**
I give my life to the Pot-   ter's   hand.

G   **D/F♯**   **Am**   **Bm7/E** **Em7**
Call me, guide me, lead me, walk beside   me;

 F   **C/E** **Am** **G/B** **Am** **G/B** **C/D**
I give my life to the Pot-   ter's   hand.

Tag

(*last time* - **F**   **C/E** **Am/D** **C/D** **G**)
           I give my life to the Pot-   ter's hand.

The Stand

Words and Music by
JOEL HOUSTON

You stood be-fore ___ cre - a - tion, ___

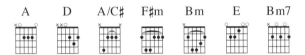

A   D   A/C♯   F♯m   Bm   E   Bm7

Verse 1

  A   **D**
You stood before creation, forever within Your hand.
A/C♯   **F♯m**   **D**
You spoke all life into motion, my soul now to stand.
A
You stood before my failure
    D
And carried the cross for my shame.
   A/C♯   **F♯m**   **D**
My sin weighed upon Your shoulders, my soul now to stand.
           D **Bm**   **F♯m**
So what can I say?   And what can I do
           D   **E**   **F♯m**
But offer this heart, oh God,   completely   to You?

Verse 2   **A**   **D**
          So I'll walk upon salvation, Your Spirit alive in me,
               A/C♯   **F♯m**   **D**
          My life to declare Your promise, my soul now to stand.
                    D   Bm   **F♯m**
          So what can I say?   And what can I do
                    D   E   **F♯m**
          But offer this heart, oh God,   completely   to You?
                    D   Bm   **F♯m   A**
          So what can I say?   And what can I do
               Bm7   E   D   A
          But offer this heart, oh God,   completely   to You?

Interlude   **E   F♯m   D   A   E   F♯m**

Chorus   **D   A   E   F♯m   D**
              So I'll stand with arms high and heart abandoned,
              A   E   F♯m   D
          In awe of the One who gave it all.
              A   E   F♯m
          I'll stand, my soul, Lord, to You surrendered.
          D   A   E   (F♯m)
          All I am is Yours.

The Wonderful Cross

Words and Music by
CHRIS TOMLIN, J.D. WALT
and JESSE REEVES

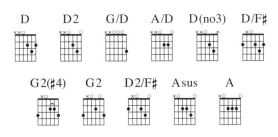

Verse 1

D		D2	D	D2	D	G/D	D	D2	D
When I sur- vey the won- drous cross

| D | | | G/D | D | D2 | D | A/D | D | D2 |
On which the Prince of Glo-ry died,

| D | | D2 | D | D2 | D | G/D | D | D2 | D |
My richest gain I count but loss,

| | D2 | D | D2 | D | D2 | D(no3) |
And pour contempt on all my pride.

Verse 2

| D | | | D2 | D | D2 | D | G/D | D | D2 | D |
See, from His head, His hands, His feet,

| D | | G/D | D | D2 | D | A/D | D | D2 |
Sorrow and love flow min-gled down.

| D | | D2 | D | D2 | D | G/D | D | D2 | D |
Did e'er such love and sor- row meet,

| | D2 | D | D2 | D | D2 | D |
Or thorns compose so rich a crown?

Chorus

D/F♯	G2(♯4)	G2	D2/F♯

Oh, the won- derful cross,

D/F♯	G2(♯4)	G2	D2/F♯

Oh, the won- derful cross

D/F♯	G2(♯4)	G2

Bids me come and die

D2/F♯	D/F♯	Asus	A

And find that I may truly live.

D/F♯	G2(♯4)	G2	D2/F♯

Oh, the won- derful cross,

D/F♯	G2(♯4)	G2	D2/F♯

Oh, the won- derful cross,

D/F♯	G2	D/F♯

All who gather here by grace draw near

Asus	A	(D)

And bless Your name.

Verse 3

D	D2	D	D2	D	G/D	D	D2	D

Were the whole realm of na- ture mine,

D	G/D	D	D2	D	A/D	D	D2

That were an of- f'ring far too small.

D	D2	D	D2	D	G/D	D	D2	D

Love so a- maz-ing, so di- vine,

D2	D	D2	D	D2	D

Demands my soul, my life, my all!

Trading My Sorrows

Words and Music by
DARRELL EVANS

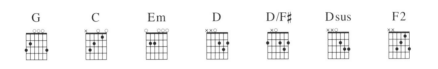

I'm trad-ing— my sor-rows, —

G	C	Em	D	D/F♯	Dsus	F2

Chorus
    G   **C**   **Em** **D** **G**   **C**   **Em** **D**
    I'm trading my sor- rows,   I'm trading my shame,

    G   **C**   **Em**   **D**   **G** **C** **Em** **D**
    I'm laying them down for the joy of the Lord.

    G   **C**   **Em** **D** **G**   **C**   **Em** **D**
    I'm trading my sick- ness,   I'm trading my pain,

    G   **C**   **Em**   **D**   **G** **C** **Em** **D**
    I'm laying them down for the joy of the Lord.

Channel
    G   **C**   **Em**   **D**
    Yes, Lord, yes, Lord, yes, yes, Lord;

    G   **C**   **Em**   **D/F♯**
    Yes, Lord, yes, Lord, yes, yes, Lord;

    G   **C**   **Em**   **D**   **G** **C** **Em** **D**
    Yes, Lord, yes, Lord, yes, yes, Lord, Amen.

Verse   **G**   **C**   **Em** **D**

I am pressed but not crushed, persecuted, not abandoned,

G **C**   **Em** **D**

 Struck down, but not destroyed;

  G   **C**   **Em**   **D**

I am blessed beyond the curse, for His promise will endure,

    G **C** **Em** **D**

That His joy's gonna be my strength.

D   **Dsus** **D**

 Though the sorrow may last for the night,

  F2   **C**

His joy comes in the morning.

Tag   **G** **C** **Em** **D**

Lai, lai, lai, lai, lai, lai, lai, lai, lai, lai, lai;

   G **C** **Em** **D**

Lai, lai, lai, lai, lai, lai, lai, lai, lai, lai, lai;

   G   **C**

Lai, lai, lai, lai, lai, lai, lai,

Em   **D** **G** **C** **Em** **D** **(G)**

Lai, lai, lai, lai, lai, lai.

Unchanging

Words and Music by
CHRIS TOMLIN

Melody:

Great is__ Your faith - ful - ness.__

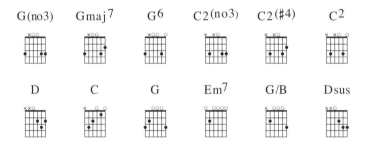

Verse 1 **G(no3) Gmaj7 G6 G(no3) Gmaj7 G6**
Great is Your faithful- ness.
C2(no3) C2(♯4) C2 C2(no3) C2(♯4) C2
Great is Your faithful- ness.
D   C
You never change. You never fail,
   G(no3) Gmaj7 G6 G(no3) Gmaj7 G6
O God.

Verse 2 **G(no3)** **Gmaj7** **G6** **G(no3)** **Gmaj7** **G6**
True are Your promis- es.
C2(no3) **C2(♯4)** **C2** **C2(no3)** **C2(♯4)** **C2**
True are Your promis- es.
D   **C**
You never change. You never fail,
   G(no3) **Gmaj7** **G6** **G**
O God.

Chorus   **Em7**   **G**   **C**   **Em7**
So we raise up holy hands to praise the Holy One
           C   **D**   **G**
Who was and is and is to come.
                  Em7   **G**   **C**   **Em7**
Yeah, we raise up holy hands to praise the Holy One
           C   **D**   **G**
Who was and is and is to come.

Verse 3 **G(no3)** **Gmaj7** **G6** **G(no3)** **Gmaj7** **G6**
Wide is Your love and grace.
C2(no3) **C2(♯4)** **C2** **C2(no3)** **C2(♯4)** **C2**
Wide is Your love and grace.
D   **C**
You never change. You never fail,
   G(no3) **Gmaj7** **G6** **G**
O God.

Bridge **Em7**   **C**   **G/B**   **Dsus**
         You were.   You are.   You will always be.

Today Is the Day

Words and Music by
LINCOLN BREWSTER and PAUL BALOCHE

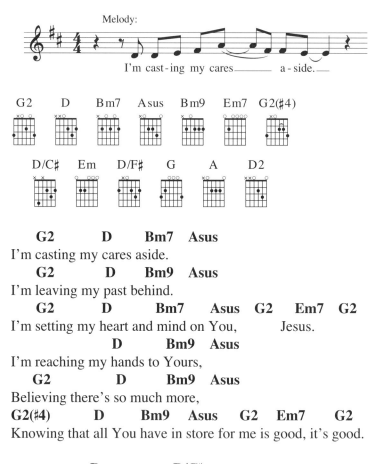

Verse 1

      G2   **D**   **Bm7**   **Asus**
I'm casting my cares aside.
      G2   **D**   **Bm9**   **Asus**
I'm leaving my past behind.
      G2   **D**   **Bm7**   **Asus** **G2**   **Em7** **G2**
I'm setting my heart and mind on You,   Jesus.
                  D   **Bm9**   **Asus**
I'm reaching my hands to Yours,
      G2   **D**   **Bm9**   **Asus**
Believing there's so much more,
G2(♯4)   **D**   **Bm9**   **Asus** **G2**   **Em7**   **G2**
Knowing that all You have in store for me is good, it's good.

Chorus

              D   **D/C♯**
Today is the day You have made.
      Bm7   **G2**
I will rejoice and be glad in it.
              D   **D/C♯**
Today is the day You have made.
      Bm7   **G2**
I will rejoice and be glad in it.

Chorus
(cont.)

Em   **D/F♯**
And I won't worry about tomorrow;
     G   **A**
I'm trusting in what You say.
           D   **Bm7**   **Asus**
Today is the day.
     G2   **D**   **Bm7**   **Asus**
Today is the day.

Verse 2   **G2**   **D**   **Bm7**   **Asus**
I'm putting my fears aside.
     G2   **D**   **Bm9**   **Asus**
I'm leaving my doubts behind.
     G2   **D**   **Bm7**   **Asus**   **G2**   **Em7**   **G2**
I'm giving my hopes and dreams to You,   Jesus.
           D   **Bm9**   **Asus**
I'm reaching my hands to Yours,
     G2   **D**   **Bm9**   **Asus**
Believing there's so much more,
G2(♯4)   **D**   **Bm9**   **Asus**   **G2**   **Em7**   **G2**
Knowing that all You have in store for me is good, it's good.

Bridge   **D**
I will stand upon Your truth. (I will stand upon Your truth.)
     D
And all my days, I'll live for You.
   D
(All my days, I'll live for You.)
     D2
And I will stand upon Your truth.
 D2
(I will stand upon Your truth.)
              Em   **G**
And all my days, I'll live for You. (All my days, I'll live.)

Final
Chorus

         D   **D/C♯**
Today is the day You have made.
    Bm7   **G2**
I will rejoice and be glad in it.
         D   **D/C♯**
Today is the day You have made.
    Bm7   **G2**
I will rejoice and be glad in it.
   Em   **D/F♯**
And I won't worry about tomorrow.
   G   **A**
I'm giving You my fears and sorrows.
Em   **D/F♯**
Where You lead me, I will follow;
   G   **A**
I'm trusting in what You say.
        D **Bm7** **Asus**
Today is the day.
  G2   **D** **Bm7** **Asus**
Today is the day.
  G2   **D** **Bm7** **Asus**
Today is the day.
  G2   **D** **Bm7** **Asus**   **G2**   **D2**
Today is the day.   Today is the day.

We Fall Down

Words and Music by
CHRIS TOMLIN

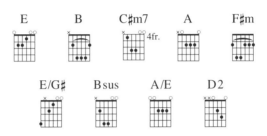

Chorus

    E   **B**   **C♯m7**   **A**   **F♯m**
We fall down, we lay our crowns at the feet of Jesus,

    E   **B**   **C♯m7**   **A**   **B**
The greatness of mercy and love at the feet of Jesus.

     E/G♯ **A**   **E/G♯** **F♯m**
And we cry holy, holy,   holy,

     E/G♯ **A**   **E/G♯** **F♯m**
And we cry holy, holy,   holy,

      C♯m7 **B**   **A**   **E/G♯** **F♯m**
And we   cry holy, holy,   holy
Bsus **B** **E** **A/E** **E** **D2** **(E)**
Is   the Lamb.

Worthy Is the Lamb

Words and Music by
DARLENE ZSCHECH

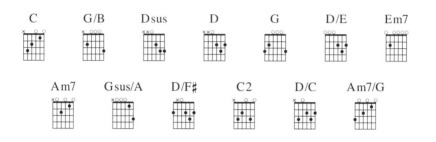

Verse

                C   **G/B**
Thank You for the cross, Lord.

                C   **Dsus**   **D** **G**
Thank You for the price You   paid.

              D/E   **Em7**
Bearing all my sin and shame,

       D   **C**   **Am7** **G/B** **Dsus**   **D**
In love You came and gave   amazing grace.

G   **Gsus/A** **G/B**   **C**   **G/B**
Thank You   for this love, Lord.

                C   **Dsus**   **D** **G**
Thank You for the nail-pierced   hands.

              D/E   **Em7**
Washed me in Your cleansing flow,

       D   **C**   **Am7**   **G/B** **Dsus** **D/F♯**
Now all I know, Your forgiveness and embrace.

Chorus   **G**   **D/F♯** **Am7** **G/B** **C2** **C**

Worthy is the Lamb, seated on the throne.

D   **D/C**   **G/B**   **C**

Crown You now with many crowns,

     Am7   **Am7/G** **D** **D/F♯**

You reign victori-   ous.

G   **D/F♯** **Am7** **G/B** **C2** **C**

High and lifted up,   Jesus, Son of God,

     D   **D/C**   **G/B** **C** **Dsus**

The Darling of heaven, cruci-   fied.

       Am7   **G/B** **C**

Worthy is the Lamb,

       Am7   **G/B** **Dsus**

Worthy is the Lamb.

Tag   **Am7**   **G/B** **C**

Worthy is the Lamb,

       Am7   **G/B** **Dsus**

Worthy is the Lamb,

       Am7   **G/B** **Dsus** **D** **G**

Worthy is the Lamb.

You Are God Alone

(Not a god)

Words and Music by
BILLY JAMES FOOTE
and CINDY FOOTE

Capo 1st fret and play in G

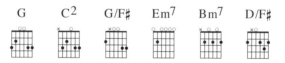

Verse 1

> G   C2
> You are not a god created by human hands.
> G   C2
> You are not a god dependent on any mortal man.
> G   G/F♯   Em7   C2   G
> You are not a god in need of anything we can give.
>   D/F♯   Bm7   C2
> By Your plan, that's just the way it is.

Chorus   G   D/F♯
          'Cause You are God alone from before time began.
                              Em7   C2
          You were on Your throne, and You were God alone.
                              G   D/F♯
          And right now, in the good times and bad,
                              Em7   C2
          You are on Your throne. You are God alone.
                              G   D/F♯
          You're unchangeable. You're unshakable.
                              Em7
          You're unstoppable.
                              C2
          That's what You are.
                              G   D/F♯
          You're unchangeable. You're unshakable.
                              Em7
          You're unstoppable.
                              C2
          That's what You are.

Verse 2   G   C2
          You're the only God whose power none can contend.
          G   C2
          You're the only God whose name

          And praise will never end.
          G   G/F♯   Em7
          You're the only God who's worthy
          C2   G
          Of everything we can give.
                     D/F♯   Bm7   C2
          You are God; that's just the way it is.

You Are Good

Words and Music by
ISRAEL HOUGHTON

A   E/A   G/A   D/A   D   E/D   Dm7   F/D

G/D   E   G   A/C♯   Em7   F2   G2

A5   C5   D5   G5   D/F♯   F5   E5

Verse   **A**

Lord, You are good

          E/A   **G/A   D/A**

And Your mercy endureth forever.

A   **E/A**   **G/A   D/A**

Lord, You are good and Your mercy endureth forever.

D   **E/D**

People from every nation and tongue,

Dm7   **F/D   G/D**

From generation to gen-   eration.

Chorus   **A**   **E** **G**   **D**
We worship You. Hallelujah! Hallelujah!
      A   **E**   **G** **D**
We worship You for who You are.
      A   **E** **G**   **D**
We worship You. Hallelujah! Hallelujah!
     A/C♯ **Em7**   **F2** **G2**
We worship You for who You are,
              A
And You are good.

Interlude   **A5** **C5** **D5**
                 Yes, You are, yes, You are, yes, You are!
A5 **G5** **D/F♯**   **F5**   **E5**
           So good, so good!

Bridge   **F5** **E5**   **A5** **C5**   **D5**
You are good,   all the time.
              A5 **C5**   **D5**
All the time,   You are good.

You Are Holy
(Prince of Peace)

Words and Music by
MARC IMBODEN
and TAMMI RHOTON

Melody:

You are   ho - ly. ___

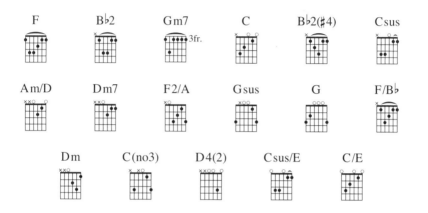

F   B♭2   Gm7   C   B♭2(♯4)   Csus

Am/D   Dm7   F2/A   Gsus   G   F/B♭

Dm   C(no3)   D4(2)   Csus/E   C/E

Verse
(Ladies echo
Men's part)

         F   **B♭2**
You are holy. You are mighty.

      Gm7   **C**
You are worthy, worthy of praise.

        F   **B♭2**   **Gm7**
I will follow; I will listen; I will love You

C   **F**   **C**   **F**
All of my days. (all of my days.)

Chorus
(Ladies sing lyrics in italics)

B♭2(♯4)   **B♭2**   **C**   **Csus**
I will sing   to   and   wor-   ship
You are Lord of   lords, You are King of kings,

Am/D **Dm7**   **F2/A**
The   King   who is   wor- thy.
You are mighty God, Lord of everything.

B♭2(♯4)   **B♭2**   **C**   **Csus**
And I   will love   and a-   dore   Him,
You're Em-manu-   el, You're the Great I AM,

Am/D **Dm7**   **F2/A**
And I   will bow   down be- fore   Him.
You're the   Prince of Peace who is the Lamb.

B♭2(♯4)   **B♭2**   **C**   **Csus**
And I   will sing   to   and   wor- ship
You're the   Living   God, You're my saving grace.

Am/D **Dm7**   **F2/A**
The   King   who is   wor-   thy.
You will reign forever, You are Ancient of Days.

B♭2(♯4)   **B♭2**   **C**   **Csus**
And I   will love   and a- dore   Him,
You are Alpha,   Omega, Beginning and End.

Am/D **Dm7**   **Gsus**   **G**
And I   will bow   down be-   fore   Him.
You're my Savior,   Messiah,   Redeemer and Friend.

B♭2
You're my Prince of Peace,

      C   **F** **(F/B♭** **Csus** **C)**
And I will live my life for You.

Tag
Dm   **B♭2**
You're my Prince of Peace,

C(no3)
And I will live my life for You.

D4(2) **Dm** **Csus/E** **C/E**   **B♭2** **B♭2(♯4)** **B♭2** **(F)**
Oh,   oh,   oh.

You Never Let Go

Words and Music by
MATT REDMAN
and BETH REDMAN

Melody:

E - ven though I   walk   through the val - ley

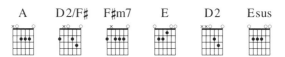

A   D2/F♯   F♯m7   E   D2   Esus

Verse 1

                    A
Even though I walk through the valley

Of the shadow of death,
         D2/F♯
Your perfect love is casting out fear.
                    A
And even when I'm caught in the middle

Of the storms of this life,
         D2/F♯
I won't turn back; I know You are near.

Pre-
Chorus
                        F♯m7   E   A
And I will fear no e-   vil,
                    F♯m7   E   A
For my God is with   me.
                    F♯m7   E   A
And if my God is with   me,
                    E   **D2**
Whom then shall I fear? Whom then shall I fear?

Chorus   **A**
Oh no, You never let go,

Through the calm and through the storm.
F♯m7
Oh no, You never let go in every high and every low.
Esus
Oh no, You never let go.
D2   **A**   **Esus** **D2**
Lord, You never let go of me.

Verse 2   **A**
And I can see a light that is coming

For the heart that holds on,
   D2/F♯
A glorious light beyond all compare.
               A
And there will be an end to these troubles,

But until that day comes,
   D2/F♯
We'll live to know You here on the earth.

Bridge   **A**
Yes, I can see a light that is coming

For the heart that holds on.
          F♯m7
And there will be an end to these troubles,
               Esus
But until that day comes,   still I will praise You.
D2   **A**   **Esus** **D2**
  Still I will praise You.

Tag   **Esus**   **D2**   **A**
Lord, You never let go of me.

You Are My King

(Amazing Love)

Words and Music by
BILLY JAMES FOOTE

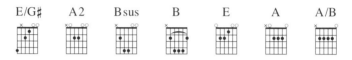

E/G♯   A2   Bsus   B   E   A   A/B

Verse   **E/G♯   A2   Bsus   B**
          I'm forgiven because You were forsaken.
          E/G♯   A2   Bsus   B
          I'm accepted;   You were condemned.
          E/G♯   A2   Bsus   B
          I'm alive and well, Your Spirit is within me
          A2   B   E
Because You died and rose again.

Chorus   **E   A**
          Amazing love, how can it be
          E   Bsus   B   A/B
          That You, my King, would die for me?
          E   A
          Amazing love, I know it's true;
          E   Bsus   B   (A/B)
          It's my joy to honor You.
          A   B   E
In all I do   I honor You.

Bridge   **E**
          You are my King, You are my King.

          Jesus, You are my King. Jesus, You are my King.

You're Worthy of My Praise

Words and Music by
DAVID RUIS

Melody:

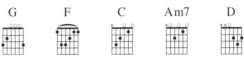

I will wor-ship (I will wor-ship)

G   F   C   Am7   D

Verse 1

G   F
I will worship with all of my heart.
C   G   Am7   D
I will praise You with all of my strength.
G   F
I will seek You all of my days.
C   G   Am7   D
I will follow all of Your ways.

Chorus

G   D
  I will give You all my worship,
C   Am7   D
  I will give You all my praise.
G   D
  You alone I long to worship,
C   Am7   D   G
  You alone are worthy of my praise.

Verse 2

G   F
I will bow down and hail You as King.
C   G   Am7   D
I will serve You, give You everything.
G   F
I will lift up my eyes to Your throne.
C   G   Am7   D
I will trust You, trust You alone.

Your Grace Is Enough

Words and Music by
MATT MAHER

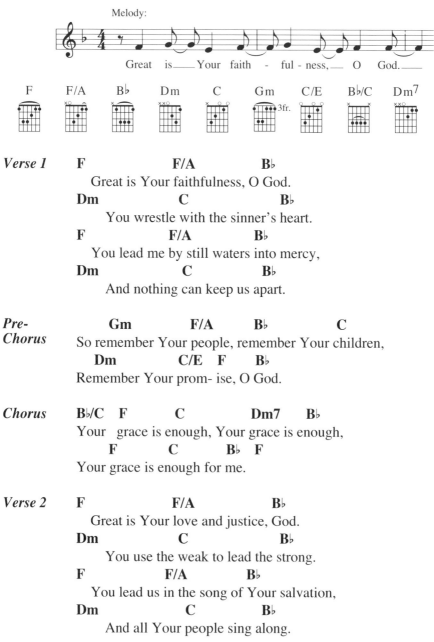

Melody:

Great is__ Your faith - ful - ness,__ O God.__

F   F/A   B♭   Dm   C   Gm   C/E   B♭/C   Dm7

Verse 1
    F   **F/A**   **B♭**
       Great is Your faithfulness, O God.
Dm   **C**   **B♭**
       You wrestle with the sinner's heart.
F   **F/A**   **B♭**
       You lead me by still waters into mercy,
Dm   **C**   **B♭**
       And nothing can keep us apart.

Pre-
Chorus   **Gm**   **F/A**   **B♭**   **C**
       So remember Your people, remember Your children,
       Dm   **C/E F**   **B♭**
       Remember Your prom- ise, O God.

Chorus   **B♭/C F**   **C**   **Dm7**   **B♭**
       Your   grace is enough, Your grace is enough,
         F   **C**   **B♭**   **F**
       Your grace is enough for me.

Verse 2
    F   **F/A**   **B♭**
       Great is Your love and justice, God.
Dm   **C**   **B♭**
       You use the weak to lead the strong.
F   **F/A**   **B♭**
       You lead us in the song of Your salvation,
Dm   **C**   **B♭**
       And all Your people sing along.

Your Love, Oh Lord

Words and Music by
TAI ANDERSON, BRAD AVERY,
DAVID CARR, MARK LEE
and MAC POWELL

Melody:

Your love, oh Lord, —

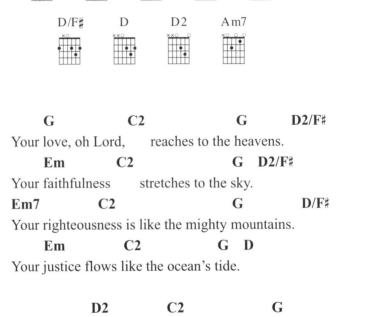

G   C2   D2/F♯   Em   Em7

D/F♯   D   D2   Am7

Chorus

G	C2		G	D2/F♯

Your love, oh Lord,   reaches to the heavens.

Em   **C2**   **G** **D2/F♯**

Your faithfulness   stretches to the sky.

Em7   **C2**   **G**   **D/F♯**

Your righteousness is like the mighty mountains.

Em   **C2**   **G** **D**

Your justice flows like the ocean's tide.

Verse

D2   **C2**   **G**

I will lift my   voice to worship You, my King.

D2   **C2**   **Am7** **D**

I will find my   strength in the shadow of Your wings.

Tag

G   **C2**   **G**   **D/F♯**

Your love, oh Lord,   reaches to the heavens.

Em   **C2**   **G**

Your faithfulness   stretches to the sky.

Your Name

Words and Music by
PAUL BALOCHE
and GLENN PACKIAM

Melody:

As morn-ing dawns and eve-ning fades,

C/E F2 G C(no3) Am7 Em7 C Gsus

Verse 1

      C/E   F2   G   C(no3)
As morning dawns and evening fades,
C/E F2 G   C(no3)
You inspire songs of praise
      C/E   F2   G   Am7
That rise from earth to touch Your heart
    F2 G   C(no3)
And glori-fy Your name.

Chorus

      Em7 Am7   C   F2
Your name   is a strong and mighty tower;
   G Am7   C   F2
Your name   is a shelter like no other.
   G Am7   C   F2
Your name,   let the nations sing it louder,
    C/E   F2   Gsus G   C/E
'Cause nothing has the power to save   but Your name.

Verse 2

C/E F2   G   C(no3)
Jesus, in Your name we pray,
C/E   F2   G   C(no3)
Come, and fill our hearts today.
    C/E F2   G   Am7
Lord, give us strength to live for You
   F2 G   C(no3)
And glori-fy Your name.

A

B

C

D

E

F